HEALTH CARE ISSUES, COSTS AND ACCESS

HOSPITAL READMISSIONS

COMPLEXITIES, REDUCTION EFFORTS, AND ANALYSES OF HOSPITAL-ACQUIRED CONDITIONS

HEALTH CARE ISSUES, COSTS AND ACCESS

Additional books in this series can be found on Nova's website under the Series tab.

Additional E-books in this series can be found on Nova's website under the E-book tab.

HEALTH CARE ISSUES, COSTS AND ACCESS

HOSPITAL READMISSIONS

COMPLEXITIES, REDUCTION EFFORTS, AND ANALYSES OF HOSPITAL-ACQUIRED CONDITIONS

STEPHAN R. COX
EDITOR

New York

Library of Congress Cataloging-in-Publication Data

ISBN: 978-1-62417-283-0

Published by Nova Science Publishers, Inc. † New York

HEALTH CARE ISSUES, COSTS AND ACCESS

HOSPITAL READMISSIONS

COMPLEXITIES, REDUCTION EFFORTS, AND ANALYSES OF HOSPITAL-ACQUIRED CONDITIONS

STEPHAN R. COX
EDITOR

NOVA BIOMEDICAL

New York

For permission to use material from this book please contact us:
Telephone 631-231-7269; Fax 631-231-8175
Web Site: http://www.novapublishers.com

Library of Congress Cataloging-in-Publication Data

ISBN: 978-1-62417-283-0

Published by Nova Science Publishers, Inc. + New York

Contents

Preface

Nearly 20% of Medicare beneficiaries aged 65 and over who were admitted to a hospital in 2005 were readmitted within 30 days following their initial discharge. The Medicare Payment Advisory Commission estimated that these readmissions cost the Medicare program as much as $15 billion per year and that perhaps as much as two-thirds of these readmissions may be preventable. This book provides an overview on the subject of hospital readmissions with a focus on the complexities, reduction efforts and analyses of hospital-acquired conditions. Hospital readmissions are associated with a number of factors and are not necessarily attributable to problems with the quality of patient care, but strong evidence indicates specific interventions to better manage care transitions at the time of hospital discharge could reduce readmissions for certain conditions.

Chapter 1 - Nearly 20% of Medicare beneficiaries aged 65 and over who were admitted to a hospital in 2005 were readmitted within 30 days following their initial discharge. The Medicare Payment Advisory Commission (MedPAC) estimated that these readmissions cost the Medicare program as much as $15 billion per year and that perhaps as much as two-thirds of these readmissions may be preventable. Many policymakers believe that different care transition programs coupled with payment reforms can constrain hospital readmissions among Medicare's fee-for-service (FFS) beneficiaries, could improve patient care, and may generate cost savings for the program. Hospital readmissions are associated with a number of factors and are not necessarily attributable to problems with the quality of patient care, but strong evidence indicates specific interventions to better manage care transitions at the time of hospital discharge could reduce readmissions for certain conditions.

Medicare is building on past work by Quality Improvement Organizations (QIOs) to help providers identify the underlying causes of hospital readmissions in their communities and then develop different strategies to prevent those rehospitalizations. In their newest round of Medicare contracts, which began August 1, 2011, QIOs will work to reduce readmissions 20% by 2013 and provide technical assistance to participants in the Community Care Transitions Program (CCTP), a $500 million, five-year demonstration program established by the Patient Protection and Affordable Care Act (ACA as amended, P.L. 111-148) to help participating hospitals improve discharge procedures and manage patients' care transitions more effectively. CCTP may be continued or expanded if the Office of the Actuary (OACT) certifies that the expansion would reduce Medicare spending without reducing quality. By mid-March 2012, 30 sites had been selected.

As well as establishing CCTP, ACA included several payment initiatives to encourage FFS providers, particularly hospitals, to work to minimize rehospitalizations and coordinate patient care across settings. Two initiatives in particular are discussed in this report, the Hospital Readmission Reduction Program (HRRP) and bundled payments. The HRRP will penalize an acute care hospital with higher than expected readmission rates by as much as 1% of its base payments starting in FY2013. Initially, the HRRP must use the three existing readmission measures that are endorsed by the National Quality Forum (NQF) and are included on Medicare's Hospital COMPARE website (where publically reported data can be used to assess hospital performance). Hospitals and industry advocates have expressed concerns about the existing measures and the effect of the readmission penalties on certain safety-net hospitals; issues that are likely to attract significant Congressional attention as the program's implementation date approaches. CMS is also exploring bundled payment methods where a single payment is made for a defined group of services rather than individual payments for each service. The national bundled payment pilot program established by the Center for Medicaid and Medicare Innovation (CMMI) is a three-year project starting in 2012 that will encompass four different bundled payment models. Changing these FFS financial incentives may be Medicare's most effective strategy for addressing hospital readmissions.

This report examines the complex issue of hospital readmissions along with Medicare's ongoing efforts and future activities to reduce unnecessary readmissions.

Chapter 2 - This report continues RTI's analysis of the effects of the hospital-acquired conditions-present on admission (HAC-POA) program on utilization, with a specific focus on readmissions. The HAC-POA program was designed to improve the quality of inpatient care to Medicare beneficiaries by providing a negative financial incentive, in which inpatient prospective payment system (IPPS) cases can no longer be assigned to higher-paying MS-DRGs on the basis of reasonably preventable complications or co-morbid (CC) conditions or major complications or co-morbid (MCC) conditions that are acquired during the hospital stay. The reimbursement effects are limited to the initial or index admission only. Thus, even though the hospital may not receive a higher rate of payment for index admissions in which a HAC occurred under the HACPOA program, hospitals could receive additional payments from the Medicare program for care provided during readmissions related to the hospital-acquired condition. A recent study has found that an additional $103 million in payment would be withheld if Medicare expanded the non-payment policy to HAC-related readmissions.

Previous research has shown to varying degrees that the likelihood of readmission is greater for patients who experience adverse events than for similar patients who have no such adverse events. Ashton and colleagues (1997) conducted a meta-analysis of the relationship between early readmission rates (31 days) and inpatient processes of care and concluded that substandard care was correlated with higher readmission rates; patients who were readmitted for unplanned reasons were 55% more likely to have had poor quality of care.

Encinosa and Hellinger (2008) studied the occurrence of seven categories of Agency for Healthcare Research and Quality patient safety indicators (PSIs) among 161,004 privately insured patients undergoing surgery. These seven groups of PSIs span the 10 HAC categories included in the HAC-POA program. Excessive 90-day readmission rates, calculated as the difference between the readmission rate estimated if all patients had the PSI and the readmission rate estimated if none of the patients had the PSI, were found for four of the seven PSI groups: infections (7.7%), pulmonary and vascular problems (3.4%), acute respiratory failure (4.3%), and metabolic problems (6.3%).

Infections after surgical procedures are an important reason for early readmissions and have been the focus of a number of recent studies. Herwaldt and colleagues (2006) studied postoperative nosocomial infections associated with general, cardiothoracic, and neurosurgical procedures in a large tertiary care medical center and associated VA hospital. They found that the risk adjusted odds ratio of being readmitted within 30 days of surgery ranged across the three surgical services from 2.15 to 5.62 for patients with a SSI compared with patients with no SSI.

Friedman and colleagues (2009) used an all payer data set of hospitalizations for surgical procedures from seven states and found that the relative risk of readmission was higher for patients experiencing at least one of nine PSIs. The unadjusted rate of 3-month readmission was 25% among patients with a positive PSI compared with 17% among those without a positive PSI. Risk adjustment reduced the 3-month readmission rate differences yet the rates remained statistically higher for patients with each of the nine PSIs.

The most recent literature points to a similar relationship between hospital-acquired conditions and readmissions. Morris et al. (2011) considered unplanned 30-day same-hospital readmissions among 1,808 surgical patients in an urban, tertiary hospital in FY 2009 and found that deep vein thrombosis significantly increased the probability of a readmission, with an odds ratio of 4.7. The reasons for readmission among these patients, however, did not seem to be related to the deep vein thrombosis.

In: Hospital Readmissions
Editor: Stephan R. Cox
ISBN: 978-1-62417-283-0

Chapter 1

Addressing Medicare Hospital Readmissions*

Sibyl Tilson and Geoffrey J. Hoffman

Summary

Nearly 20% of Medicare beneficiaries aged 65 and over who were admitted to a hospital in 2005 were readmitted within 30 days following their initial discharge. The Medicare Payment Advisory Commission (MedPAC) estimated that these readmissions cost the Medicare program as much as $15 billion per year and that perhaps as much as two-thirds of these readmissions may be preventable. Many policymakers believe that different care transition programs coupled with payment reforms can constrain hospital readmissions among Medicare's fee-for-service (FFS) beneficiaries, could improve patient care, and may generate cost savings for the program. Hospital readmissions are associated with a number of factors and are not necessarily attributable to problems with the quality of patient care, but strong evidence indicates specific interventions to better manage care transitions at the time of hospital discharge could reduce readmissions for certain conditions.

Medicare is building on past work by Quality Improvement Organizations (QIOs) to help providers identify the underlying causes of

---

* This is an edited, reformatted and augmented version of a Congressional Research Service publication, CRS Report for Congress R42546, from www.crs.gov, prepared for Members and Committees of Congress, dated May 25, 2012.

hospital readmissions in their communities and then develop different strategies to prevent those rehospitalizations. In their newest round of Medicare contracts, which began August 1, 2011, QIOs will work to reduce readmissions 20% by 2013 and provide technical assistance to participants in the Community Care Transitions Program (CCTP), a $500 million, five-year demonstration program established by the Patient Protection and Affordable Care Act (ACA as amended, P.L. 111-148) to help participating hospitals improve discharge procedures and manage patients' care transitions more effectively. CCTP may be continued or expanded if the Office of the Actuary (OACT) certifies that the expansion would reduce Medicare spending without reducing quality. By mid-March 2012, 30 sites had been selected.

As well as establishing CCTP, ACA included several payment initiatives to encourage FFS providers, particularly hospitals, to work to minimize rehospitalizations and coordinate patient care across settings. Two initiatives in particular are discussed in this report, the Hospital Readmission Reduction Program (HRRP) and bundled payments. The HRRP will penalize an acute care hospital with higher than expected readmission rates by as much as 1% of its base payments starting in FY2013. Initially, the HRRP must use the three existing readmission measures that are endorsed by the National Quality Forum (NQF) and are included on Medicare's Hospital COMPARE website (where publically reported data can be used to assess hospital performance). Hospitals and industry advocates have expressed concerns about the existing measures and the effect of the readmission penalties on certain safety-net hospitals; issues that are likely to attract significant Congressional attention as the program's implementation date approaches. CMS is also exploring bundled payment methods where a single payment is made for a defined group of services rather than individual payments for each service. The national bundled payment pilot program established by the Center for Medicaid and Medicare Innovation (CMMI) is a three-year project starting in 2012 that will encompass four different bundled payment models. Changing these FFS financial incentives may be Medicare's most effective strategy for addressing hospital readmissions.

This report examines the complex issue of hospital readmissions along with Medicare's ongoing efforts and future activities to reduce unnecessary readmissions.

Introduction

Policy-makers and patient advocates are concerned that Medicare patients are cycling in and out of acute care hospitals too frequently and that high hospital readmission rates may be a marker of poor quality of care.[1] Nearly

20% of Medicare beneficiaries aged 65 and over who were hospitalized in 2005 were readmitted within 30 days following their initial hospital discharge. The Medicare Payment Advisory Commission (MedPAC) estimated that these readmissions cost $15 billion per year in hospital payments and that as much as two-thirds of these readmissions may be preventable.[2] As Medicare hospital stays have become shorter and beneficiaries' post-acute care becomes more fragmented, the movement of inpatients out of hospitals into other health care settings and the transition of Medicare beneficiaries between different post-acute providers have been identified as areas that need attention. In MedPAC's view, existing incentives to coordinate care across providers and settings are limited, because Medicare pays each provider separately and because payments to these providers are not affected by their ability or efforts to coordinate care across settings. In fact, under the existing fee-for-service (FFS) payment system, hospitals that devote resources to reducing readmissions may suffer financially (unless other patients fill the unused beds). Changes that address hospital readmissions among Medicare's FFS beneficiaries, such as placing a greater emphasis on effective discharge planning, adoption of different care management programs, and payment reforms, may improve patient care and generate cost savings for the program.[3]

The implementation of these changes becomes more complicated because readmission rates,[4] the use of post-acute services,[5] and hospital utilization in general,[6] vary substantially among geographic locations. Communities with higher admission rates tend to have higher readmission rates and perhaps a greater dependence on hospitals as a site of care.[7] Also, the type of post-acute care (if any) a beneficiary receives after the initial discharge can vary and may affect readmission rates. After a hospital stay, roughly 40% of Medicare beneficiaries are discharged to a post-acute setting providing skilled nursing care or rehabilitation services. Rates of 30-day hospital readmissions among beneficiaries discharged to skilled nursing facilities (SNFs) have been increasing over time; almost one-quarter of the Medicare beneficiaries discharged from a hospital to a SNF in 2006 were readmitted to the hospital within 30 days.[8] MedPAC has found that the risk-adjusted rate at which Medicare covered SNF patients with any of five potentially avoidable conditions (congestive heart failure, respiratory infection, urinary tract infection, sepsis and electrolyte imbalance) were rehospitalized in 2009 was 14.2%, with considerable variation among SNFs.[9] Under current Medicare FFS payment rules, hospitals and post-acute providers lack financial incentives to address hospital readmissions by coordinating beneficiaries' care, improving clinical information sharing, ensuring appropriate placement across the range of different post-acute settings, or addressing other inefficiencies across providers.[10]

Hospitals must comply with standards established by Medicare's Conditions of Participation (COP) to bill the program. Medicare's COP requires hospitals to have a discharge planning process that applies to all patients. Under existing regulations, hospitals are expected to evaluate whether a patient is expected to experience adverse health consequences upon discharge, develop a discharge plan and arrange for its initial implementation, and counsel the patient, family members or interested parties about the availability of post-hospital care. However, hospital discharge planning is viewed as limited in scope and influence on patient behavior. (Other factors associated with rehospitalizations and the effectiveness of hospital discharge planning are discussed in *Appendix A*.) Transitional care models are intended to supplement the existing hospital discharge planning process, provide patients with services both prior to discharge and after discharge from the hospital, and often emphasize targeting care for "vulnerable" chronically ill patients (those who are older, in poor health, or who have been hospitalized previously) most at risk for hospital readmission. [11]

Generally, a readmission is seen as an outcome that is preceded by a number of intermediary events that, in certain circumstances, may be addressed and remedied. From August, 2008 through July, 2011, as part of their 9th Statement of Work (SOW) Medicare's Quality Improvement Organizations (QIOs) in 14 states have been assessing primary factors affecting readmissions to develop interventions to target these factors. In their view, the causes of readmission include:

- Fragmented documentation of medical conditions or failure to communicate need for medical treatment;
- Poor patient self-management;
- Inadequate follow-up in the post-discharge setting;[12]
- Community infrastructure and awareness problems;
- Insufficient patient support, including support from family caregivers; and
- Medication discrepancies that occur during an initial admission or following a discharge and which may result in illness or harm to a patient.

QIO's work-to-date suggests readmissions can be reduced by bringing together community stakeholders to create standardized processes to support patients before and after discharge from the hospital. Other QIO readmission efforts have focused on improvements to patient and caregiver education, medication management, or use of common patient health records to improve communication of patient health information between providers within and outside the hospital setting. As discussed later in "Current Medicare Care Transition Initiatives," QIOs efforts to address readmissions are continuing in their 10th SOW.[13] QIOs are also providing technical assistance to candidates seeking to participate in the Community Care Transitions Program established by the Patient Protection and Affordable Care Act (ACA as amended, P.L. 111-148).

This report is intended to help Congress understand the complex issue of hospital readmissions and Medicare's ongoing and future activities to address those rehospitalizations.[14] To that end, the next sections of the report will discuss factors that may influence hospital readmissions, Medicare's readmission measures, existing payment incentives for FFS reimbursement and the existing hospital COPs. The report will then discuss Medicare's efforts to provide technical and financial assistance to hospitals' efforts to improve discharge procedures and manage patients' care transitions. The final section of the report will discuss Medicare's upcoming payment initiatives to address hospital readmissions, specifically the Hospital Readmission Reduction Program (HRRP) and the bundled payment demonstrations currently proposed by the Center for Medicare and Medicaid Innovation (CMMI).[15]

Factors that Influence Hospital Readmissions

There is an ongoing debate in the academic literature and among industry advocates about which factors influence hospital readmissions, and whether and how much control hospitals have over these underlying factors. The challenge facing Medicare in attempting to reduce hospital readmissions is to provide appropriate incentives, including targeted technical assistance, to encourage hospitals to address the underlying causes and then work to minimize rehospitalizations, particularly since readmissions generate additional Medicare payments for hospitals. Medicare's efforts are further complicated by a large body of research which identifies possible causes that are associated with readmissions, with limited consensus about which should be included for a fair assessment of hospital performance. The following discussion examines some of the research on these factors, including a description of the mixed evidence of their importance.

Generally, research has found that Medicare beneficiaries with certain medical conditions and demographic characteristics are more likely than others to be readmitted to the hospital after a discharge. Medicare FFS claims data from 2003 to 2004 indicate that readmission rates range broadly by condition and procedure. More than three-quarters of all rehospitalizations occurred after initial admissions for medical conditions, not surgical conditions. Most rehospitalizations (regardless of whether the initial admission was for a surgical or a medical condition) were for medical conditions.[16] Relatively high readmission rates are found for Medicare beneficiaries with multiple chronic illnesses.[17,18,19] An additional factor that may be associated with readmissions is a patient's history of prior rehospitalizations.[20] Patients with worse health—as indicated by higher clinical severity scores—have higher 30-day readmission rates than patients with lower severity scores. The differences in these readmission rates between the two groups have increased over time.[21]

Demographic characteristics, such as race, age, gender, and socio-economic status have been studied as factors influencing the likelihood of readmissions, with mixed results.[22] The different studies of readmission risk factors varied by the target condition(s) included, analytic approach, follow-up period, and handling of deaths and hospital transfers among other features.[23] Generally, across a number of studies assessing the significance of various risk factors for hospital readmission, there is no evidence that demographic characteristics like age, gender, or factors such as income or education consistently predict hospital readmissions.[24] There is some evidence indicating variation in readmission rates by race and socio-economic status, cited by advocates who wish to have those factors reflected in the readmission models.[25,26,27] One study examined the readmission rates of black and elderly Medicare patients receiving care at minority-serving hospitals (defined as inclusion in the top ten percent of hospitals by proportion of black patients served) and non-minority serving hospitals from 2006 to 2008. It found that older black Medicare patients had higher readmission rates than white patients for three common medical conditions: acute myocardial infarction (AMI), congestive heart failure (CHF)[28], and pneumonia (PN), but concluded that the association of readmission rates with the site of care was consistently greater than the association with race.[29]

Some have cautioned that the inclusion of certain non-clinical factors, such as race and socioeconomic status, should be avoided in statistical models used for the public reporting of health outcomes, because these factors may be related to patient quality of care that are important to capture and for hospitals to address.[30] One concern is that including an adjustment for race or socioeconomic status lowers the performance bar for hospitals that serve a high proportion of these patients and does not provide comparable incentives to work to minimize readmissions as other hospitals. Alternatively, hospital advocates maintain that, without such an adjustment, safety-net hospitals serving these patient populations will be disproportionately affected and the resulting financial penalties (when the hospitals may already be financially strained) could reduce quality of care provided to such patient populations. Also, in their view, without such a risk adjustment, other hospitals may have an incentive to avoid treating minority and low-income patients if those populations are seen as having higher readmission rates. Simply stated, it can be difficult to assess whether the high readmission rates associated with certain categories of patients should be attributed to them or the hospitals that they predominantly use.

As an additional complication, patients may not properly manage their own health conditions or use of medications and thus may be at risk for readmissions. The post-discharge period is a "vulnerable phase" for patients who may have worsening clinical conditions; without appropriate support from family members or caregivers, patients discharged from the hospital may not follow through with nutrition and diet, medication usage, and other therapies.[31] A patient who is discharged from the hospital but does not see a primary care provider outside the hospital, may be susceptible to readmission if the patient's condition deteriorates and there is no adequate follow-up care.[32] These situations may be mitigated if the physician who treated the patient in the hospital communicates with the patient's primary care physician or other family members, but this does not occur routinely.[33] Moreover, families of patients may not know what post-acute care options are available to them.[34] Alternatively, available, accessible options for post-acute or follow-up care may be limited within certain communities.

Certain hospital processes and procedures could be implicated in readmissions. For instance, a hospital that does not properly assess the medications a patient was taking prior to admission may unknowingly prescribe a medication which has an interaction with one of the patient's existing medications; this could lead to an adverse event and result in a readmission. In other instances when diagnostic information or the treatment course provided to the patient during the hospitalization is not recorded, the patient's primary care provider outside the hospital may not be able to correctly diagnose or assist with the patient's condition.[35] Additionally, communication by hospital staff and physicians to patients within the hospital is important—better patient satisfaction scores at hospitals (including patient satisfaction with discharge planning, for heart failure and pneumonia, but not for AMI) are associated with lower risk-adjusted 30-day readmission rates.[36]

Finally, hospitals currently do not have financial incentives to avoid rehospitalizations or to delay discharges.[37] Under the current FFS system, Medicare does not reimburse for supportive services for patients (including those with complex medical conditions) even if such activities may reduce readmissions. Medicare also does not pay hospitals or other providers for transitional care services, another activity thought to reduce readmissions. For example, hospitals and other providers may not provide telephone reminders about follow-up medical appointments, medication reminders, in-home check-ups, or care coordination with outpatient providers on behalf of the patient post-discharge because these extra services are not rewarded and result in extra costs for hospitals or other providers.[38] Additionally, shorter lengths of stay under Medicare's FFS payment system have been posited as an explanation for higher readmission rates; however, compared to higher-cost hospitals, lower-cost hospitals (which are likely to discharge patients earlier) do not have significantly higher 30-day readmission rates.[39]

Although certain studies indicate that readmission rates are associated with age, patient illness, and other factors, the specific reasons such persons are readmitted may warrant continued investigation. A variety of adverse events might occur before a hospital admission, during a hospital stay, as a patient is being discharged, or after a patient is home or in another setting that could result in rehospitalization. The reasons for readmission likely vary by person, by hospital, and by care setting, if not by locality.

Medicare's Readmission Measures

The Centers for Medicare & Medicaid Services (CMS) has drawn increased attention to the topic of hospital readmissions by establishing readmission measures for three common Medicare hospitalizations as quality indicators and including that data on its Hospital COMPARE website to permit public assessment of hospitals' performance in this area. The readmission measure for patients treated for heart failure (HF) was finalized in the FY2009 inpatient prospective payment system (IPPS) rule published in the *Federal Register* on August 19, 2008;[40] the two other measures for readmitted patients treated initially for AMI and PN were finalized in the CY2009 hospital outpatient final rule published November 18, 2008, after endorsement of the measures by the National Qualify + (NQF).[41] Starting June, 2009, Hospital COMPARE indicates whether a hospital's risk-adjusted relative 30-day hospital readmission rates for Medicare patients initially admitted for HF, AMI, and PN were higher, lower, or no different than the U.S. national average.[42] Beginning in FY2010, CMS's Inpatient Quality Reporting (IQR) program also included the readmission data used to construct risk-adjusted 30-day readmission rates for these Medicare patients as quality measures.[43] Accordingly, since then, the amount that a hospital's inpatient payment rate is increased each year could depend upon reporting the required quality data on readmission measures. [44]

As discussed in *Appendix B*, the three readmission models estimate hospital-specific, risk-standardized, all-cause 30-day readmission rates for patients discharged alive to a non-acute care setting with a principal diagnosis of HF, AMI, and PN. The measures include admissions to all short-stay acute-care hospitals for people age 65 years and older who are in FFS Medicare and who have a complete-claims history for 12 months prior to admission. The measures are risk-adjusted to account for Medicare patients' age, gender, past medical history, and other diseases, conditions or comorbidities that increase readmission risks.[45] The three condition-specific readmission measures are adjusted for patient-level risk factors and account for a hospital quality of care effect using hierarchical regression modeling techniques.[46] The FY2012 IPPS final rule indicates that CMS has adopted the same three measures for comparing hospital's readmission rates under the HRRP established by Section 3025 of ACA.[47] Under this program, hospitals with higher-than-expected spending on readmissions for Medicare FFS beneficiaries initially hospitalized with one of these three principal diagnoses will be penalized starting in FY2013. The penalty will be capped at 1% of a hospital's base payments for all its Medicare discharges in FY2013, 2% in FY2014, and 3% in FY2015 and subsequently.

CMS has established its three readmission measures as all-cause readmissions of an aged beneficiary to the same hospital or a different hospital within 30 days of the original (index or initial) admission, with limited exclusions of subsequent admissions. [48] Academics, other policy makers, and organizations have used different time periods and definitions to measure readmissions. [49] Also, unlike an all-cause measure, other approaches to readmission measures attempt to identify preventable admissions and use different methods to distinguish those readmissions that might be avoided and those that might not be avoided. As noted by certain hospitals and their advocates, these different methods can result in different relative readmission rates for hospitals, a comparative analyses that may have financial implications for their Medicare payments starting in FY2013 when the penalties are implemented. Also, although Medicare's all-cause readmission measures do exclude certain readmissions, according to hospital advocates they do not exclude a sufficient number of planned readmissions related to the original admission or, as directed by statute, a sufficient number of unrelated readmissions.[50] Finally, hospital advocates fear that the HRRP program may end up penalizing hospitals unfairly for those factors affecting readmissions that are out of their control. This is expressed as a particular concern for safety-net hospitals that serve challenging patient populations within limited financial if not clinical resources. However, as discussed subsequently, CMS has implemented other policy initiatives and demonstration projects to provide technical and financial assistance to address fundamental causes of rehospitalizations, particularly for certain low-performing providers.

Medicare's Existing Payment Incentives and Conditions of Participation (COP) for Discharge Planning

Policy makers have longstanding concerns about the financial and quality incentives in a FFS payment system. Generally, under FFS, a provider receives a payment, set in advance, for each service, bears the risk for the number and costs for inputs that comprise that service, but has no limit on the number of services provided. Most typically, payment is made regardless of quality or outcomes.[51] The current design of Medicare's IPPS for acute care hospitals in particular (and FFS generally) does not provide incentives to hospitals to contain avoidable readmissions for beneficiaries or to improve the quality of care provided.[52] Medicare now pays for all readmissions except when patients are rehospitalized within 24 hours after discharge for the same condition for which they were originally hospitalized.[53] Under existing payment incentives, hospitals could lose income by reducing readmissions, as fewer rehospitalizations would result in fewer billable discharges. Under Medicare FFS, hospitals and physicians are usually paid separately, even if a physician is working in the hospital. In fact, although IPPS hospitals are usually paid on a per-case basis, physicians are typically paid on a per-service basis. Similarly, post-acute care providers of post-hospital care are each paid separately and receive more reimbursement for each Medicare admission or episode of home health care.

Under IPPS, Medicare pays for most acute-care hospital stays using a prospectively determined payment for each discharge, intended to cover the services provided during a hospital stay;[54] any differences between Medicare payments and hospital costs, either profits or losses, are absorbed by the hospital. In essence, hospitals are financially rewarded for the efficient delivery of medical and surgical care and are more likely to discharge patients earlier.[55] These incentives to provide efficient care also extend to the amount of resources that hospitals dedicate to discharge planning. Hospitals that participate in the Medicare program are required by Medicare's COP to provide discharge care instructions to Medicare beneficiaries.[56] These requirements are subject to survey and recertification efforts by state agencies or by CMS-approved accrediting bodies.

The Medicare discharge-planning COP regulation (42 CFR 482.43) requires Medicare participating hospitals (more than 90% of all acute-care hospitals in the United States) to have a discharge planning process that applies to all patients. The hospital is required to identify all patients who are expected to experience adverse health consequences upon discharge at an early stage of hospitalization. The hospital must provide a discharge-planning evaluation to these patients and to other patients upon request; this evaluation must be done on a timely basis and must include an evaluation of the patient's likely need for and availability of post-acute services. This information must be included in the patient's medical record and the hospital must discuss the evaluation results with the patient or patient's representative. The hospital must develop any necessary discharge plan and arrange for its initial implementation.[57] The hospital must counsel the patient, family members or interested parties as necessary to prepare them for post-hospital care and advise them of its availability.[58] The hospital must transfer or refer patients along with necessary medical information to appropriate facilities, agencies, or outpatient services as needed for follow-up or ancillary care.

Despite these requirements, some studies have found instances in which discharge planning is incomplete and necessary information is not provided by hospitals to physicians and post-acute providers in a timely manner. A literature review of 55 observational studies published between 1970 and 2005 indicated that primary care physicians considered the following information to be among the most important components of discharge information: a patient's main diagnosis; pertinent physical findings; results of procedures and laboratory tests; and discharge medications, with reasons for any changes to the previous medication regimen; among other information.[59] However, these studies also found that audits of hospital discharge documents, which are often physician-dictated and transcribed, demonstrated a frequent absence of such information. In addition, only between 12% and 34% of physicians treating a patient after a hospital discharge had a copy of the patient's hospital discharge summary.[60] Another analysis of discharge summaries of adults 70 years and older at an academic teaching facility found that 74% of summaries did not include pending test results and 82% of the summaries did not include information regarding patient's final cognitive status.[61] Generally, outpatient physicians who do not have complete and timely information about a patient's case may not make adequate follow-up care decisions.

The evidence regarding the impact of hospital discharge planning activities as now conducted on hospital readmissions may depend upon measures used to assess discharge planning. A study used two different discharge planning measures to evaluate CHF and PN readmissions. [62] It found no association between CHF readmission rates and a measure based on whether discharge planning was documented in the medical record chart. [63] (As noted by the author, this measure may simply capture whether hospitals document their activities, not the adequacy of the process or the sufficiency of the information conveyed to patients, caregivers, and post-acute providers.) There was only a modest association between PN and CHF readmissions and a readmission measure based on the patient-reported experience with discharge planning. In fact, there was only a weak correlation between the two discharge measures.[64]

As discussed in the next section, there is a body of work that supports the importance of comprehensive and timely discharge planning as a strategy to reduce hospital readmissions. A meta-analysis of 8 studies of HF patients receiving comprehensive discharge planning, which generally entails post-discharge activities, had 75% the risk of hospital readmission compared to patients with HF treated with usual care.[65] A systematic review of 21 randomized controlled trials with patients having a mix of medical and surgical conditions found that patients with an individualized discharge plan, compared to those without an individualized discharge plan, had 85% of the readmission risk.[66] In its June 2011, report, MedPAC recommended that the hospital COP be updated to encourage the adoption of different processes that are thought to improve patient outcomes. For instance hospitals could be required to get discharge instructions to the appropriate community provider within 48 hours of discharge (which is thought to reduce hospital readmission rates).[67] On October 24, 2011, CMS published proposed changes to the hospital (and critical access hospital) COP, primarily to streamline burdensome or dated regulations. These regulations were finalized on May 16,

2012 and become effective July 16, 2012. There were no modifications to the existing hospital discharge planning requirements.

The following section will discuss recent and ongoing efforts to identify certain systemic causes and structured approaches to address Medicare rehospitalizations within specific providers and communities, including the recently implemented pilot project, the Community Based Care Transitions Program.

Current Medicare Care Transition Initiatives

Prior to the enactment of ACA, from August 2008, through July 2011, during its 9th SOW, QIOs in 14 states collaborated with providers in selected communities to identify the underlying causes of hospital readmissions in their communities and then develop different strategies to prevent those rehospitalizations.[68] QIOs sought to identify causes of poor transitional care and to develop targeted intervention strategies in order to improve patient outcomes, such as reducing 30-day readmission rates. The Care Transitions Quality Improvement Organization Support Center (QIOSC)—which assisted Medicare QIOs in the care transition project— found three fundamental causes of patient readmissions: (1) declining health conditions that were not being properly managed, (2) medication regimens that were not appropriate, and (3) inappropriate use of emergency rooms (rather than using other types of medical services).[69] The QIOSC attributed these problems to three systemic gaps in care for patients:[70]

- Lack of engagement or activation of patients and families into effective post-acute self management,
- Lack of standard and known processes among providers for transferring patients and medical responsibility, and
- Ineffective or unreliable sharing of relevant clinical information.

To address these gaps, QIOs worked on different approaches to (1) engage (or activate) patients;[71] (2) develop standard, known discharge processes, including scheduling necessary follow-up care;[72] and (3) ensure that clinicians and providers have necessary, timely information on the patient's condition and need for follow-up care.[73] *Table 1* provides a brief summary of underlying causes of hospital readmissions, their significance for readmissions as well as specific interventions thought to address those contributing factors. This information is supplemented by the discussion in *Appendix A* of this report.

Table 1. Causes of and Tools for Addressing Readmissions

Problem	Goal	Significance for readmissions	Specific interventions to address problem
Fragmented documentation - Diagnostic test results, hospital treatment information, tests pending at discharge, or follow-up plans—which are considered essential by physicians treating discharged patients—are often not provided in hospital discharge summaries.	Improve discharge planning – Provide clear, timely, understandable information or instructions regarding patients' likely need for post-hospital treatment, as well as post-acute treatment options to all patients or their representatives. Develop standardized approaches to providing appropriate discharge planning for patients at risk for rehospitalization.	Future hospitalizations may be reduced, in part, by informing patients and caregivers in a timely manner about how best to manage the patient's care following hospital discharge, as well as regarding availability of post-acute providers in the geographic area.	1) Create a patient health record. 2) Evaluate the hospital discharge plan. 3) Communicate with providers in the hospital to discuss tests and patient care plan.
Poor patient self-management - Many patients may not receive information they need to manage their care. For instance, heart failure patients did not receive information about worsening symptoms, diet, drug interactions, follow-up appointments, and weight monitoring.	Educate patients on self-management of care – Teach patients and their representatives how to manage and advocate for their health care needs to prevent the unnecessary decline of patient health and/or address the appropriate interventions for the patient's health.	Patient behavior could contribute to risks for future hospitalizations, due to inappropriate use of medications, poor understanding of signs of deteriorating health, or other poor management.	1) Make follow-up appointments and coordinate referrals for community resources. 2) Discuss test and laboratory results with patients. 3) Assist patients with understanding prescribed medications. 4) Coach patients to advocate for their own health needs and to recognize health warning signs. 5) Follow-up with patients after discharge, including home visits and telephone calls.
Lack of post-discharge follow-up - Many patients are not meeting with a physician outside the hospital setting following hospital discharge. In	Improve post-acute follow-up and patient support - Provide access and reminders to patients and their representatives to necessary post-acute care,	Information regarding patient treatment history or post-discharge plans may not be available to the post-acute	1) Make follow-up appointments and coordinate referrals for community resources. 2) Create a patient health record. 3)

Problem	Goal	Significance for readmissions	Specific interventions to address problem
addition, a large proportion of patients are not receiving discharge instructions. Around 25% of Medicare beneficiaries are reported to have been rehospitalized following a stay in a skilled nursing facility (SNF).	including rehabilitative, home health, or skilled nursing services. Fill in communication gaps between hospital and other providers by ensuring sharing of appropriate clinical information.	providers— including home health agencies, physicians, or SNFs—resulting in treatment errors or poor care.	Support self-management. 4) Use bundled payment methodology.
Community infrastructure problems - Substantial variation among states in regard to hospital readmission from SNFs has been observed. Variation among states has also been observed in regard to hospital readmissions.	Bring together community stakeholders - Create awareness of the readmissions issue and begin to address practice patterns that may contribute to readmissions.	In part due to different regional practice patterns, compared to areas with fewer hospital beds, areas with more hospital beds may be more likely to have higher hospital readmission rates.	State-specific programs that 1) bring together various state-level and local stakeholders to identify and apply community resources; and 2) partner hospitals with patients, home health agencies, SNFs and outpatient providers.
Lack of patient support - Patients who live alone or have no access to caregiver support are more at risk for a hospital readmission than those with a support system.	Improve caregiver engagement and education to create a support system for the patient in the post-discharge setting - Enable caregivers to understand and comply with discharge care plans, including taking patients to follow-up physician visits or other appointments, or by assisting with patients' other daily needs.	Assistance provided by caregivers may help prevent the occurrence of an adverse event or the deterioration of patient health that may lead to a rehospitalization.	1) Educate caregivers about warning signs of deteriorating patient health. 2) Involve caregivers in discussion of post-discharge follow-up needs. 3) Educate caregivers, along with patients, about patient care needs and disease management.
Medication discrepancies - Medication errors are some of the most widespread medical errors and may be common in hospitals. Also, surgical errors have been shown to be associated with a higher risk of hospital readmission.	Establish common personal health record and reconcile medication - Provide a tool with personalized information about medications used by patient as well as reconcile pre-hospital visit medication list with discharge medication list.	Medication discrepancies can lead to adverse events, which can lead to an emergency room and/or a hospital readmission.	Perform medication reconciliation in hospital. Educate patients about medications. 3) Create and use patient health record. 4) Maintain telephone contact (or visit homes of patient) to address medication issue.

Source: CRS summary of QIO documents and readmission literature available at http://www.cfmc.org/integratingcare/toolkit.htm.

As part of the 10th SOW which began August 1, 2011, QIOs will work to reduce readmissions 20% by 2013 which would prevent the rehospitalization of an estimated 1.6 million hospital patients, among other goals.[74] QIOs will also provide technical assistance to candidates seeking to participate in Community Care Transitions Program (discussed next) and other communities.[75]

Community-Based Care Transitions Program (CCTP) for High-Risk Medicare Beneficiaries

Section 3026 of the ACA establishes a five-year community-based care transitions program (CCTP) for eligible entities beginning January 1, 2011, to test models for improving care transitions for high-risk Medicare beneficiaries.[76] An eligible entity is an IPPS hospital with high readmission rates[77] or certain community based organizations (CBOs)[78] that provide care transition services. Consideration is given to CBOs working with multiple high readmission hospitals in the community. Preference is given to entities that participate in the care transitions program administered by the AoA or that provide services to medically underserved populations, small communities, and rural areas. Consideration is given to physician practices (particularly primary care practices) that meet the statutory CBO definition, to programs that have established care management interventions with state Medicaid programs and those who have established relationships with primary care medical homes serving Medicare beneficiaries (described subsequently). As noted by CMS, awardees are expected to work closely with accountable care organizations (ACOs) and medical homes developed in their communities, as it is ultimately the responsibility of the delivery system to manage care transition and the services needed to support them.

The goals of the CCTP are to improve transitions of high-risk beneficiaries from the inpatient hospital setting to other care settings, to improve quality of care, to reduce readmissions for high-risk beneficiaries, and to document measureable savings to the Medicare program. To this end, Medicare plans to spend $500 million for this five-year program beginning in January 1, 2011. CCTP may be continued or expanded if the Office of the Actuary (OACT) certifies that the expansion would reduce Medicare spending without reducing quality.[79]

CMS has published a solicitation for applications from entities interested in participating in the CCTP.[80] CCTP applications must describe the root cause analysis that informed the selection of the proposed intervention and target population. These applications also include information about the beneficiary notification process which tells them about participation in the program and information about the applicant's implementation strategy (including recruitment strategy and contingency plans for achieving beneficiary participation thresholds). Applicants must have prior experience with successfully managing care transitions and reducing readmissions. Entities are awarded a two-year agreement that may be extended—based on their performance—on an annual basis for the remaining three years. Applicants must provide a budget and a per eligible discharge rate for transitional care services. Entities selected to participate are paid a per eligible discharge rate to cover the direct costs of care transition services, and are paid by CMS on a monthly basis for services delivered in the previous month. [81]

CMS has selected the Lewin Group, a health care consulting organization, to provide support to entities selected to provide transitional care services. The Lewin Group and its team will provide technical assistance and guidance for an estimated 500 CBOs and hospitals expected to be involved in the project. Lewin will gather best practices through site visits and facilitate peer-topeer information sharing through online collaboration and national meetings.[82] On November 18, 2011, CMS made the first seven site selections for CCTP. An additional 23 sites were selected to participate in CCTP on March 14, 2012. [83] Other awards will be issued on a rolling basis until the $500 million funding ceiling is reached.

The statutory language establishing the CCTP indicated that the care transition interventions could include 1) initiating transition services no later than 24 hours prior to discharge, 2) arranging timely post-discharge follow-up to educate patients and caregivers about responding to their own health symptoms, 3) providing assistance to ensure productive and timely interactions between patients and post-acute and out-patient providers, 4) providing self-management support (or caregiver support), and 5) conducting medication review, counseling, and management support. The intervention may not include payment for discharge planning services required under Medicare COP.

In the CTTP solicitation, CMS provides information about certain evidence-based care transitions models that were jointly funded by AoA and CMS. Entities participating in the program are not required to use these transition models,[84] but consideration is given to applicants proposing to use the following care transition models:[85]

- The Care Transitions Initiative (CTI) is a four-week program which provides a nurse transition "coach" (an advanced practice nurse) to assist patients with complex care needs, and their families, in being more assertive during care transitions, to have continuity of care across settings, and have their needs met in any care setting. [86] In a randomized controlled trial involving 750 subjects aged 65 and older in a large, integrated delivery system in Colorado, patients receiving the CTI had lower readmission rates at 30 days and at 90 days and lower mean hospital costs than those patients without the CTI intervention.[87] In addition, a qualitative review of the results appeared to indicate improved self-management and confidence about what was required by study participants who received the intervention.[88] A number of hospitals and health systems have implemented the CTI model, including the implementation of CTI in 2007 in 10 California locations as part of a one-year, $650,000, effort funded by the California Health Care Foundation.[89]
- The Transitional Care Model (TCM) created by a team based at the University of Pennsylvania (including testing in three completed National Institutes of Health funded randomized, controlled clinical trials), establishes a transitional care team led by an advanced practice nurse who has a masters degree in nursing. This transitional care nurse (TCN) treats a patient before, during, and after discharge from the hospital and specifically targets chronically ill high-risk older adults.[90] In a multi-site randomized control trial for persons age 65 and older and hospitalized with heart failure, the intervention TCM group had fewer readmissions in one year following hospital discharge. The total cost of care for the intervention group was 39% lower per patient than for the control group.[91]
- Project BOOST (Better Outcomes for Older Adults through Safe Transitions) has a toolkit which aims to improve care transitions for older adults. [92] The intervention sponsored by the Society of Hospital Medicine and the John A. Hartford Foundation, involves a risk assessment of the patient on eight dimensions with risk-specific interventions developed to target specific patients.[93] The patient's understanding of his or her situation as well as readiness to be discharged is assessed at different points during the hospital stay.[94] Project BOOST is associated with improved quality of life, increased involvement and satisfaction with hospital discharge care and improved communication between the hospital and physicians.[95]

- Re-Engineered Design (RED) consists of a set of 11 actions taken primarily during a hospital stay by discharge advocates (registered nurses) to address care transition elements. [96] In a study involving Project RED, 370 patients participating in the project were one-third less likely to be readmitted to the hospital or visit the emergency department than patients who did not participate in the project. Compared to roughly one-third of patients not in the project who left the hospital with a follow-up appointment, almost all project participants had an appointment at that time. Also, more than 90% of participants' primary care physicians received patient discharge information within one day of leaving the hospital. Medication review by pharmacists of project participants also successfully identified a number of medication errors.[97] and
- Transforming Care at the Bedside (TCAB) was created through a partnership between the Institute for Healthcare Improvement and the Robert Wood Johnson Foundation in 2003 in order to address safety and quality of patient care in hospitals and to improve staff satisfaction. One aspect of TCAB addresses transitional care and encompasses (1) assessing the patient's post-discharge options *at the time of hospital admission*; (2) educating the patient and family caregiver and confirming their understanding of discharge instructions; (3) providing medication information to outpatient providers seen after leaving the hospital; and (4) scheduling post-acute care follow-up for high-risk patients,[98] or providing a follow-up phone call and scheduled physician office visit to moderate risk patients. [99] An assessment found the intervention was associated with reductions in patient wait times and an increase in patient and staff satisfaction, among other benefits.[100]

Generally, these models aim to provide (1) care coordination between the hospital and post-hospital settings and providers; (2) education of patient and family caregivers; (3) follow-up monitoring of a patient's health status after discharge; and (4) care from a transitional coach or team to manage clinical, psychosocial, rehabilitative, nutritional, and pharmacy needs after discharge. The scope of the intervention (and therefore the associated costs) with respect to patients targeted, as well as the duration and types of services involved, will vary by care transition model. *Table 2* summarizes key features of the five different care transition models.

Table 2. Key Features of Five Different Care Transition Models

	Care Transitions Initiative (CTI) "Coleman Model"	Transitional Care Model (TCM) "Naylor Model"	Project BOOST	Re-Engineered Design (RED)	Transforming Care at the Bedside (TCAB) Creating an Ideal Transition Home
Program focus	Patient/caregiver coaching and education. Patient self-management.	Discharge management and follow-up.	In-hospital and discharge management and follow-up.	Discharge management and follow-up.	Discharge management. Patient self-management and follow-up.
Patients Targeted					
Age	Age 65 and older (may be applied to younger adults).	Age 65 and older.	At least 18 years old, with a focus on older adults.	No age specified.	No age specified.
Risk factors and other patient characteristics	Have at least one of 1 1 diagnoses. English speaking with working telephone. Planned discharge to home or SNF (not long-term care).	2 or more risk factors: recent hospitalizatio ns, multiple chronic conditions, or poor self-health ratings. Patient's home is primary care setting (testing TCM on longterm care recipients).	Identifies high risk patients using 8P screening tool at admission.	Not discussed.	Moderate-risk and high-risk patients with congestive heart failure (but can be adapted and generalized to other patient populations).
Assessment of cognitive ability and ability to participate in intervention	Cognitive ability and mental state determined through mental health screen. For patients who fail or if dementia is present, a willing, reliable caregiver is	Cognitively intact patients are required (are now testing TCM on cognitively impaired older adults).	Cognitive ability assessed on admission. If dementia is present, then a reliable caregiver is required.	Not discussed.	Patient assessment on admission, including cognitive status. Goal is to identify learner(s) who can be either patient or caregiver.

	Care Transitions Initiative (CTI) "Coleman Model"	Transitional Care Model (TCM) "Naylor Model"	Project BOOST	Re-Engineered Design (RED)	Transforming Care at the Bedside (TCAB) Creating an Ideal Transition Home
	required.				
Program Scope					
Length of program	4 weeks.	1-3 months.	Hospital admission up to 72 hours after discharge.	Hospital admission up to 72 hours after discharge.	Hospital admission up to 5 days following discharge.
Staff or team involved	Transitions "coach" does not provide skilled care.	Transitions care nurse (TCN) is an advanced practice nurse (APN) with masters degree and a caseload of 15-20 patients.	No explicit care coordinator. Team approach among clinical nursing staff, hospitalists (physicians who specialize in the practice of hospital medicine) and other hospital staff.	Trained registered nurse ("discharge advocate") coordinates discharge plan with the hospital team.	Teams of 5-7 people, including front-line staff (nurses, physicians, and pharmacists) and patients or caregivers to create hospital program; APN makes follow-up phone calls.
Patient education	Educates patients or caregivers about medications and personal health record. Provides information about signs of deteriorating conditions and appropriate follow-up actions.	Educates patients and caregivers to identify (and meet) health goals and manage care. Nurse discusses medication and discharge instructions with patient and family.	Uses teach-back method1 with patients and caregivers to discuss medications, diagnosis, prognosis, and self-care, as well as to educate about warning signs requiring further medical attention.	Provides education throughout the hospital stay. Explains medication plan. Educates patient about medical emergency options. Assesses patient's grasp of the discharge plan and follow- up care.	Uses teaching materials (written, visual, audio, and face- to-face) and uses teach-back methods every day to educate patient and families about critical information needed after discharge.

Table 2. (Continued)

	Care Transitions Initiative (CTI) "Coleman Model"	Transitional Care Model (TCM) "Naylor Model"	Project BOOST	Re-Engineered Design (RED)	Transforming Care at the Bedside (TCAB) Creating an Ideal Transition Home
In-hospital services	One visit to help patient manage transition out of hospital.	Assessment within 24 hours of TCM enrollment. Daily visits throughout stay.	At different points of stay, patients are assessed using general assessment of preparedness (GAP) tool to see if they are ready for discharge.	Contact throughout the hospital stay.	Intervention begins in the hospital on the first day of admission and continues every day during hospitalization.
Discharge planning plan or checklist	Provides personal health record (PHR) with structured discharge checklist.	Provides written plan with instructions and phone numbers for emergency care.	Provides patients with clear, understandable written discharge instructions that have reminders of what patients must do to care for themselves following discharge.	Evaluates discharge plan compared to national guidelines. Gives the patient a written discharge plan with hospitalization, medication, and follow-up care information.	Designates team member accountable for effective discharge of each patient. Gives patient discharge checklist.
Post-discharge follow-up services with patient	Follow-up visits to SNF and/or the home. Telephone calls.	TCN visit in home within 24- 48 hours of discharge and at least weekly during the first month following discharge, and	Telephone contact within 72 hours of discharge. Ensures follow- up appointment with aftercare medical provider	Telephone contact 2-3 days after discharge to reinforce discharge plan and help with any problems.	Prior to discharge: for high risk patients, schedule face-to-face visit within 48 hours after discharge; for moderate risk

	Care Transitions Initiative (CTI) "Coleman Model"	Transitional Care Model (TCM) "Naylor Model"	Project BOOST	Re-Engineered Design (RED)	Transforming Care at the Bedside (TCAB) Creating an Ideal Transition Home
		at least semi-monthly during the rest of the intervention; daily telephone availability.	within 7 days. Arranges transportation to initial follow up.		patients, follow-up phone call within 48 hours and physician visit within 5 days.
Assistance with planning follow- up services or treatment or communicatio n with post hospital providers.	Emphasize importance of follow-up physician visit; prepare for visit using role-playing. Coach follows up with primary care provider or specialist following patient visit with provider or specialist.	TCN accompanies patient on first post-discharge physician visit and, if needed, on subsequent visits.	Hospitals confirm that patient's principal outpatient provider receives discharge summary. Suggests communicatin g discharge summary information to other post-acute providers.	Makes appointments with clinicians and for post-discharge laboratory testing and other services. Coordinates appointments and helps patients keep these appointments. Provides outpatient physicians with discharge summaries, medication lists, list of patient medical issues, including test results.	Provides patient information (discharge summaries) to next care providers within one day of discharge. Prior to discharge, schedules an office visit for moderate and high-risk patients.
Medication management services	In-hospital medications are discussed with patient and at home visit medication lists	TCN discusses medications with hospital pharmacist and other.	Medications are reconciled at admission, during in-hospital transfers and	Reconciles the discharge medication plan with prior medication plan.	Reconciles medications on admission and discharge. Evaluates withheld

Table 2. (Continued)

	Care Transitions Initiative (CTI) "Coleman Model"	Transitional Care Model (TCM) "Naylor Model"	Project BOOST	Re-Engineered Design (RED)	Transforming Care at the Bedside (TCAB) Creating an Ideal Transition Home
	are reconciled. Intervention focuses on medication self-management by patient. Medication list provided in PHR.	providers. TCN reconciles medication upon patient discharge from hospital	at discharge. Medication use and side effects are reviewed with patients.	Medication use and side effects are discussed. Plan for acquiring medications is discussed with patient.	medications to decide if necessary to restart. Provides new medication list and assesses patient's understanding of list.
Written documentation of patient's treatment, conditions and plan of care at discharge	PHR includes patients medical history, medications (dosages) and allergies, list of warning signs or "red flags" (drug reactions and signs of worsening condition).	Each patient and primary care provider of the patient receives a summary of the patient's transition, at the end of the TCM intervention	Principal care providers receive discharge summary. Patients receive printed reminders of post-discharge care plan.	Patients are given a written discharge plan	Transitionreport assesses patient's ability to engage in various self-care activities Patients are given phone numbers to call for help, reasons to request help, and self-care instructions

Source: CRS summary of information from care models' websites provided in above descriptions.

[1] Teach back involves asking patients to recall and restate what they have been told.

Among other goals, CCTP seeks to document whether Medicare can realize measurable program savings by paying for care transition services. Evaluations of the earlier Medicare Care Coordination Demonstration (MCCD) [101] or the Medicare Health Support (MHS) Pilot Program[102]did not find that care coordination programs resulted in clear improvements to patient quality of care or lower Medicare's costs. Still, an examination of the more successful MCCD participants indicates that care coordinators should interact with patients in person rather than by telephone only and should collaborate closely with patients' physicians to influence their care.[103] At this point, experts suggest that the most effective intervention for care coordination with respect to cost savings and quality improvement would include a proven care transitions program.[104] However, hospitals or other entities may face certain difficulties in implementing or sustaining care transitions initiatives. Patient participation rates in these programs have been low, as a substantial proportion of patients were not interested in enrolling in the transitions programs or receiving home visits.[105]

One study found that exposing heart failure patients to a transitions program led to a nearly 50% reduction in 30-day readmission rates. Looking at the program expenditures, hospital costs and patient revenues, the study found that the contribution of each patient to the hospital's profit margin was reduced by $227 using a care transitions program, compared to the status quo.[106] Each participating hospital lost roughly $750 of revenue on average for each patient participating in the program.[107] The authors speculate that even after implementation of the readmission penalties, hospitals still would not have a financial incentive to pay for transitions programs. In their view, potential future payment reforms, such as bundled payments or payment based on episodes of care, may be necessary to encourage integration of the delivery system along with the effective use of coordination of care and improved transitional care programs.[108]

These conclusions were supported in a cost analysis of different clinical interventions and a simulation of alternative payment incentives using data from New York state.[109] Generally, a hospital's response would depend both on its circumstances and the payment incentives established by the different payors.[110] The study examined pay-for-performance (P4P) and episode-based payments. The P4P simulation assumed that each hospital would receive a reduced payment if its readmissions exceeded a benchmark. With this payment design, a payer would retrieve savings immediately even if hospital behavior did not change because low-performing providers were paid less when they exceeded the benchmarks. High-performing hospitals' payments were not adjusted. Although high performers have no financial incentive to reduce readmissions further, low-performing hospitals were seen as having the greatest potential for reducing aggregate readmissions. In this simulation however, only 7% of low-performing hospitals respond to the payment penalty by implementing a program, such as CTI or Project RED, to reduce readmissions.[111] As discussed in the next section, the financial incentives for episode-based payments are markedly different than bundled payments under

FFS. Under episode-based payment structures as modeled in the simulation, at least half of the hospitals in New York state could be motivated to implement either CTI or Project RED.

Forthcoming Medicare Payment Initiatives to Address Readmissions

As well as establishing CCTP to assist certain high readmission hospitals with care transitions, ACA included several payment initiatives to encourage FFS providers, particularly hospitals, to work to minimize rehospitalizations, if not coordinate patient care across settings. This section will discuss the Hospital Readmission Reduction Program (HRRP), the national pilot program included in ACA, and the national bundled payment pilot program established by the Center for Medicaid and Medicare Innovation (CMMI).[112]

The Hospital Readmissions Reduction Program (HRRP)

Section 3025 of ACA establishes the HRRP which will reduce Medicare's payments to hospitals with higher than expected readmission rates starting for discharges on October 1, 2012. [113] In FY2013 and FY2014, CMS has been directed to select high-volume and high-expenditure conditions that have readmission measures that are endorsed by NQF. In FY2015, the readmission measures will be expanded (to the extent practicable) to include the additional four conditions identified by MedPAC in its June 2007, *Report to Congress* and to other appropriate conditions.[114] For those measures, the Secretary may use measures without NQF endorsement as long as due consideration is given to any endorsed measures. Under the program, acute-care hospitals with excess readmissions will have their base operating DRG payment amounts (for all Medicare discharges) reduced by an adjustment factor.[115] The adjustment factor selected is the one that would result in the least amount of penalty for the hospital. Specifically, the HRRP adjustment in a fiscal year will be the greater of: (1) a floor adjustment factor of 0.99 in FY2013; 0.98 in FY2014 and 0.97 in FY2015 and beyond or (2) an excess readmissions ratio based on a hospital's adjusted actual or predicted readmissions versus adjusted expected readmissions (which is used to calculate the amount of excess payments for the applicable conditions and then divided by the hospital's total operating base payments for Medicare to derive a penalty percentage). MedPAC has estimated that the aggregate HRRP penalties will be approximately 0.2% of Medicare's IPPS payments in 2013.

CMS is implementing this program over two years. In the FY2012 IPPS rate-setting process, CMS finalized the readmission measures and related methodology, the calculation of the readmission rates, and the public reporting of the data. While the 2012 rule included a general discussion of the payment adjustment model, specific information regarding the payment adjustment will be included in next year's IPPS rule. In FY2013, the program will include three readmissions measures for Medicare inpatient hospital readmissions involving three high-volume and/or high-rate conditions, PN, AMI, and HF, which account for approximately 12% of all Medicare admissions. As endorsed by NQF, Medicare's time frame for a readmission is 30 days.[116] As CMS stated, a 30- day timeframe incorporates "a substantial proportion of readmissions attributable to an index [or initial] hospitalization" and is short enough so that hospitals and other community entities would be able to improve patient outcomes with appropriate hospital care and transitional care.[117] For the FY2013 hospital readmission program, CMS will assess hospital performance on readmissions using a three-year measurement period (the applicable period) starting in July 1, 2008 through June 30, 2011. IPPS hospitals with a small number of cases in the selected conditions (less than 25 cases in three years) would not be subject to the HRRP penalty (but their cases would be included in the national data). Critical access hospitals and other IPPS exempt hospitals will not be subject to the readmission penalty.[118] As noted earlier, CMS did not propose specific policies with respect to the HRRP payment adjustment in the FY2012 rule, but did receive public comments on certain issues. (See the discussion of the CMS' all-cause measure in *Appendix B* for additional information on implementation issues raised during the FY2012 IPPS public comment period.)

HRRP's risk-adjustment is intended to control for differences across hospitals in patient characteristics. Some contend, however, that certain factors affecting readmissions are not accounted for in the existing risk adjustment and that some hospitals may find it more difficult than others to reduce readmission rates. Because of the patients that they treat or due to other factors, hospitals with more complex patient populations or those in certain locations, may have greater difficulty than other hospitals in responding to high readmission rates.[119] Some fear that these hospitals may have limited resources to spend investing in strategies to reduce preventable readmissions. This problem may be compounded because the payment penalty applies to only hospitals and not to other providers that may care for a patient following a patient discharge.[120] Finally, hospitals may be located in areas where access to post-acute care or supportive services within the community following a hospitalization (during the time period for measuring readmissions) is limited and thus hospitals treating patients in those areas may be less able to prevent readmissions.

Other factors confronting hospitals may compete with HRRP's incentives to reduce readmissions. First, hospitals will continue to be paid for each readmission; despite the payment penalty applied to the per discharge Medicare reimbursement, hospitals can potentially reduce losses from the penalty with income from the readmissions. Second, there are annual caps on the payment penalty, which could create an incentive for some hospitals to limit their investments in patient safety and other readmission reduction strategies if the costs of such investments are greater than the potential payment penalty.[121] Third, hospitals may be able to change coding practices, alter transfer policies or use of outpatient observation to avoid countable readmissions. For instance, hospitals could change coding practices to avoid identifying patients with AMI, HF, or PN; alternatively, hospitals might have increased incentives to transfer such initial admissions to other hospitals or readmit such patients on an outpatient basis for observation services rather than rehospitalize them.[122] Fourth, since the initial readmission rate is based only on three conditions, hospitals may elect to target Medicare patients admitted with those diagnoses (in order to minimize resources expended and perhaps any associated reduction in patient volume) rather than adopting a broadly based care transition program across all conditions and all patients. Finally, the emphasis on preventing readmissions, although laudable, may come at the expense of other quality improvement or patient safety efforts.

The final sections of this report will briefly describe the National Payment Bundling Pilot Program included in Section 3023 of ACA and then discuss the Bundled Payment for Care Improvement Initiative announced by CMMI.

National Pilot Program of Payment Bundling

Under a bundled payment method, a single payment is made for a defined group of services rather than individual payments for each service. Depending upon the scope of services included in the bundle, it may be used to pay for items or services furnished by a single provider or those furnished by several providers in different health care settings. Bundled payments are increasingly seen as a way to move away from the existing FFS incentives and to reduce Medicare costs, increase coordination of care, and improve the quality of care.[123]

As established by Section 3023 of ACA, beginning no later than January 1, 2013, a voluntary pilot program will pay a single health care entity for all services delivered during an entire care episode centered on a hospitalization. CMS has deferred implementation of this national pilot program, so few details about its design are available. Moreover, the statutory language provides only general guidance about the design of the pilot program and leaves many implementation decisions to the Secretary such as:

- Which entities can receive bundled payments?
- What is an effective payment design and rate-setting method?
- What period of time after a hospitalization should constitute an episode?
- What additional services should be included in the bundle?
- What medical conditions should be included in the pilot?
- How should quality of care be measured?
- What constitutes an adequate post-acute provider referral network? and
- What patient assessment instrument should be used?

The statutory language defines a care episode as three days prior to a hospital admission, the hospital stay, and the first 30 days following discharge (unless another time period is selected). In addition to Medicare's traditional acute and post-acute services,[124] participating providers will be expected to deliver care coordination, medication reconciliation, discharge planning, transitional care services and other appropriate services. The pilot can cover up to 10 conditions which may include a mix of chronic or acute conditions, or surgical or medical conditions. The selected conditions might be those with a significant variation in readmission or post-acute spending or those with high volume and high post-acute spending. These conditions might be deemed most suitable for bundled payments across the spectrum of care given the range of practice patterns or those where evidence indicates that costs could be reduced without affecting quality.

The pilot's payment methods may include bundled payments and bids from entities for episodes of care. An appropriate patient assessment instrument to evaluate the beneficiary's condition and ensure the most clinically appropriate post-acute site for care will be used in the pilot. Site neutral quality measures for an episode of care and for post-acute care will be developed.[125] Also, participating entities must provide an adequate choice of providers and suppliers to beneficiaries. However, payments for all services provided during the episode must meet a budget neutrality standard; spending cannot exceed an estimate of what would otherwise have been spent on these beneficiaries in the absence of the pilot. Finally, if the Secretary determines that the expansion of this program would reduce Medicare spending without reducing quality of care and the Chief Actuary for CMS certifies that such an expansion would reduce Medicare spending, the duration and scope of the pilot can be expanded after January 1, 2016.

Bundling payments for acute and post-acute care has the potential to reduce costs without compromising outcomes by changing some of the incentives within FFS Medicare. An entity's financial returns will be higher if the patient is discharged to the community earlier or uses the least costly post-acute care setting. Since the entity bears the financial risk of both a readmission and the costs of all post-acute care, there is a strong incentive to coordinate care across settings, provide necessary post-acute care in the least expensive setting and not discharge patients prematurely. However, identifying a mix of providers that will agree to share payments may be challenging for that entity, unless provider groups are already organized under a single umbrella entity. Further, whether and how well providers can deliver coordinated care across an episode remains unclear. With bundled payments, there are strong incentives to take an active role in monitoring the provision of post-hospital care which could lead to unintended adverse consequences with respect to limiting access to necessary post-acute care or restricting patients' choice of post-acute providers.[126] Moreover, bundled payments alone would not necessarily create an incentive to lower the volume of patients served because hospitals and providers could profit from additional episodes of care.

Bundled Payment for Care Improvement Initiative

CMS has made implementation decisions with respect to a separate payment bundling effort. Under its authority to test innovative payment and service delivery models, CMMI issued a request for applications in August 2011, for its Bundled Payments for Care Improvement Initiative (Bundled Payment Initiative). The three-year project starting in 2012 will encompass four different bundled payment models.[127] Generally, CMS will make one payment for the services a Medicare beneficiary receives during an episode of care. The eligible awardees (participating organizations), eligible suppliers and providers, scope of services included in the episode, and payment methods vary by model. Subject to certain standards, a participating organization may determine the conditions, length of an episode of care, target price, discount and other organizational components, including participating suppliers and providers. All models are subject to a post-episode monitoring period to ensure that that aggregate Medicare Parts A and B spending for the included beneficiaries does not increase as a result of the initiative; the awardees will pay Medicare for aggregate expenditures that exceed the trended baseline spending (based on historic claims experience including "risk threshold" set by CMS).[128] Three of the models use a retrospective bundled payment method where the participating providers and suppliers are paid for services at a negotiated discount. Two of those models will compare those payments to a target price. If below the target, the awardees may share the savings with their participating providers. If above the target, the awardees will remit the difference to CMS. In the fourth model, the participating organization will be paid a single prospectively determined bundled payment for the episode. Generally, all bundled payment models will permit gainsharing arrangements where participants will be able to share any financial benefits that occur because of the efficiencies that result from better coordinated care.[129] Mandatory participation in any gainsharing arrangement is not permitted.[130]

Table 3 illustrates the differences in eligible services included in the different bundled payment models.

In Model 1, Medicare will continue to pay acute care hospitals under IPPS, but participating hospitals will be paid a reduced amount that reflects the applicable discount percentage on all MS-DRGs. Medicare Part B payments to physicians and other practitioners are not included as part of the episode and will not change under this model. The hospital is financially responsible if aggregate Medicare Parts A and B expenditures increase beyond a threshold for the period of the inpatient stay or during the 30 days after discharge, compared to historical expenditures.

Model 2 spans the widest scope of services, from initial hospitalizations through related professional services and post-acute care (PAC) as well as care associated with related readmissions. Model 3 is similar to Model 2, but the episode begins with the first PAC service within 30 days of a patient's discharge from an IPPS hospital for an agreed upon condition. The IPPS hospitalization is not included in the Model 3 payment bundle. In Models 2 and 3, Medicare will continue to pay each provider through the traditional claims processing mechanism at the full FFS rates for the dates of service, but these payments will be retroactively reconciled with the target price. After an episode of care concludes, the aggregate Medicare expenditures for that episode of care will be compared to the target price. If the actual expenditures are less than the target price, Medicare will pay the difference. If the actual expenditures are more than the target price, the difference will be repaid to Medicare.

Table 3. Differences in Eligible Services Included in the Four Bundled Payment Models

	Model 1: Only Part A inpatient hospital care	Model 2: All inpatient care (Parts A & B) plus post-acute care	Model 3: Only post-acute care (Parts A & B)	Model 4: Only inpatient care
Care Related to the Initial Hospitalization				
Preadmission Services0	X	X		X
Initial Hospitalization[b]	X	X		X
Hospital Physician[c]		X		X
Care Provided After the Initial Discharge				
Post-acute Care (PAC) [d]		X	X	
Related Admissions[e]		X	X	X
Hospital Physicianc		X	X	X
Community Physician[f]		X	X	
Other Post-Discharge Services[g]		X	X	

Source: CRS adaption of CMS documents and Commonwealth Fund Blog on Bundled Payment Initiative.

[a] Hospital diagnostic testing and all related therapeutic Part A services furnished within 3 days of admission by an entity wholly owned or operated by the admitting hospital.

[b] Acute care hospital facility Part A services furnished during the hospital stay.

[c] All Part B physician and other professional services provided during the hospital stay.

[d] Related PAC services paid under Parts A and B, including a long-term care hospital, skilled nursing facility, inpatient rehabilitation facility, and home health agency care.

[e] Part A services for related readmissions and all related Part B services during the post-discharge period including related and unrelated readmissions.

[f] Physician and other professional services delivered in an outpatient setting including the emergency department and hospital outpatient department.

[g] Related Parts A or B services including outpatient therapy service clinical laboratory services, durable medical equipment and Part B drugs.

In Model 4, Medicare will make a single, prospectively established bundled payment to the acute-care hospital where a beneficiary is hospitalized.[131] Unlike the bundled payments under Models 2 and 3, the Model 4 episode does not include PAC services. All Part A services and Part B physicians' services furnished during the inpatient stay are included in the bundled payment, and the hospital will be responsible for distributing the payment to the other providers caring for the patient.

Payment will be based on historical spending trends for all hospital facility and professional services during the initial hospitalization and related readmissions. The awardee (whether or not it is the admitting hospital) will be financially responsible for Medicare expenditures for any related readmissions for at least 30 days. Unlike the Medicare Acute Care Episode (ACE) demonstration project, none of the program savings will be shared with beneficiaries.[132]

A participating provider will receive a bundled payment for all Medicare beneficiaries who receive care and meet the episode definition. Beneficiaries who meet the eligibility criteria and receive care from a model participant cannot opt out of the bundled payment program for that particular provider. These beneficiaries will be notified of the provider's participation and have the right to get care from a different provider who is not involved in the bundled payment initiative.

Table 4 summarizes key features of the four bundled payment models in CMMI's bundled payment initiative.

Table 4. Characteristics of the Four Bundled Payment Models under CMMI's Bundled Payment Initiative

	Model 1: Only Par A inpatient hospital care	Model 2: All inpatient(Parts A & B) plus post-acute care	Model 3: Only post-acute care (Parts A & B)	Model 4: Only inpatient care
Eligible awardees/participating organizations	Physician group practices, Inpatient prospective payment system (IPPS) hospitals, health systems, physician-hospital organizations (PHOs), and conveners.[a]	Physician group practices, IPPS hospitals, health systems, post acute care (PAC) providers, PHOs, and conveners.		Physician group practices, IPPS hospitals, health systems, PHOs, and conveners.

Table 4. (Contiued)

	Model 1: Only Par A inpatient hospital care	Model 2: All inpatient(Parts A & B) plus post-acute care	Model 3: Only post-acute care (Parts A & B)	Model 4: Only inpatient care
Target conditions	All Medicare Severity-Diagnostic Related Groups (MS-DRGs) (overlapping MS-DRGs covered by other models will not be included).	Proposed by applicants. Agreed-upon MS-DRGs for inpatient hospital stay.		
Length of episode	Inpatient stay in the acute care or IPPS hospital.	Option 1: 30 to 89 days or Option 2: a minimum of 90 days after initial discharge.	At least 30 days after initial post-acute discharge (which occurs within 30 days of discharge from an acute care hospital for an included MS-DRG).	At least 30 days from discharge.
Payment method	Discounted IPPS payment to hospital. (physician payments not included).	Traditional fee-for-service (FFS) payments to participating entities subject to reconciliation to predetermined target price.		Prospectively set bundled payment to admitting hospital. Hospital distributes payments.
	See "episode and post-episode reconciliation" row.			
Expected Medicare discount	Minimum discount of 0.0% in 1st 6 months, 0.5% in 2nd 6 months, 1.0% in 2nd year and 2% in 3rd year. Exact discount set by applicant.	Minimum discount of 3% for episodes with a post- discharge period of 30-89 days. Minimum discount of 2% for 90 day or longer episodes. Exact discount set by applicant.	Proposed by applicant.	Minimum discount of 3%. A larger discount would apply for certain MS-DRGs (covered by the ACE demonstration).
Episode and post-episode reconciliation	Parts A and B payments for the hospital stay that exceed trended	If aggregate FFS payments for included services during episode exceed a target amount, entity pays Medicare the difference. If the		Any Part B professional claims, Parts A and B claims for

	Model 1: Only Par A inpatient hospital care	Model 2: All inpatient(Parts A & B) plus post-acute care	Model 3: Only post-acute care (Parts A & B)	Model 4: Only inpatient care
	aggregate payments beyond a risk	reverse occurs, Medicare pays the difference to the participating		related re-admissions paid outside the bundled
	threshold will be repaid. Parts A and B payments over a 30 day post-hospital monitoring period that exceed a trended aggregate payments above a threshold will be repaid.	organization. Parts A and B payments over a 30 day monitoring period that exceed a trended aggregate payments above a threshold will be repaid.		payment will be repaid by the participating organization. Parts A and B payments over a 30 day monitoring period that exceed a trended aggregate payments above a threshold will be repaid.
Monitoring period	30 days post-hospital discharge.	30 days after the end of the episode.		30 days post-hospital discharge.
Quality measures	All Inpatient Quality Reporting (IQR) measures and additional measures proposed by applicant.	Proposed by applicants. At some point, CMS will establish a standardized set of measures that are aligned with other required measures.		

Source: Adapted by CRS from CMS documents.

[a] A convener is an entity such as a state hospital association or a group of providers that can bring together multiple participating health care providers.

Conclusion

Hospitals are required by Medicare's COP to have a discharge planning process that applies to all patients. However, the incentives for a hospital to expend significant resources on an effective discharge planning process within the existing Medicare FFS payment system are blunted. Medicare is striving to encourage hospitals to adopt care-transition programs and will modify FFS payment incentives so that hospitals will be more attentive to how this transition care is provided and the costs of such care. As a positive inducement, CMS is providing technical and financial assistance to hospitals to enable the adoption of care models so they can better manage the patient discharge process and address problem areas associated with hospital readmissions. Future penalties for hospitals with higher than expected readmissions may also motivate change. Since June, 2009, CMS has included comparisons of hospitals' 30-day risk-adjusted readmission rates for aged Medicare patients with AMI, HF, and PN on its Hospital Compare website. Starting in October, 2012, the importance of the publically reported data will be magnified as low-performing hospitals will be subject to readmission penalties. The adoption of bundled payment methods holds the promise of providing clear incentives to avoid service overutilization and enhance care coordination between providers. Medicare seeks to align financial and other incentives so that hospitals will proactively identify and track patient problems longitudinally, rather than treat emergent care crises after they have occurred.

On the other hand, certain issues have been raised about the level of control that hospitals have over readmissions, particularly since the FFS payment system will still reimburse the majority of providers and health care professionals for the volume of services they provide. While some hospitals will be penalized for having too many readmissions and others will be paid a bundled payment for certain services, these payment changes are limited in scope and do not correct for some of the over-riding incentives within the majority of Medicare's payment systems. Also, as noted by hospital advocates, readmissions do not depend solely on the quality of inpatient care or the extent of the care transitions services rendered to a particular beneficiary. Readmissions can be contingent on the quality and the availability of post-acute and outpatient care, an individual's access to such care, an individual's access to caregivers at home or other unique circumstances. In the view of CMS, the existing measures adjust for key factors that are clinically relevant and have strong relationships with patient outcome. The agency seeks to motivate hospitals to work with their communities to lower readmission rates and improve patient care. These initiatives are necessary first steps to understand how to address the complicated (and expensive) problem of Medicare readmissions; CMS has acknowledged the need to monitor its implementation carefully to prevent untoward impacts on beneficiary access to quality care.

Appendix A. Hospital Actions That May Mitigate Against Readmissions

The QIOs, in their 10th Statement of Work's Care Transitions Theme, and other experts in care transitions have considered a number of factors that are responsible for hospital readmissions. A discussion of selected factors is provided in this appendix.

Improving Hospital Discharge Procedures

Hospital discharge planning is intended to provide clear, timely, and understandable information or instructions to the patient and his or her caregiver or family members, as well as to other providers outside the hospital setting. This process may include addressing needed post-discharge services, medications, and equipment, setting up follow-up appointments, coordinating with families as well as providing some education to patients (and their caregivers) about the transition to home or other settings, upon discharge. Experts recommend that the discharge process within a hospital be standardized with an explicit delineation of roles and responsibilities among hospital staff to ensure that the patient leaves the hospital under the best possible circumstances and avoids adverse events that could lead to rehospitalization.[133] Ideally, the discharge process begins before the decision that the patient should be discharged is made and education of the patient and the caregiver should occur throughout the hospitalization, not just at the time of discharge. Advocates of a standardized discharge process maintain that the discharge summary should be completed before discharge and updated at time of discharge. A personalized patient health record may complement the formal hospital discharge summary and should include information regarding the patient's medications and dosages, a checklist of items to be completed by the time of discharge, questions the patient may have for providers outside the hospital setting, among others. Recently, MedPAC discussions have included adding a COP requirement that hospitals provide patients' discharge instructions to the appropriate community provider within 48 hours of discharge. This COP change has not been proposed by CMS.

Lapses in the hospital discharge planning process can lead to problems with post-discharge care and with the quality of the patient's discharge summary. Prior to discharge, a number of different hospital personnel can provide information to patients about results from laboratory tests, prescribed medications, and other clinical or therapeutic information as well as instructions about how to care for a condition and whether post-discharge follow-up care is required. Upon leaving the hospital, patients may not have a clear idea of what post-acute or community, outpatient care they require or how best to facilitate their own care.

Generally, fragmented documentation can indicate a problem with hospital discharge planning and have a significant impact on post-hospital providers' ability to render competent care. For example, a patient can be discharged from the hospital before the results of ordered tests have been completed and included in the discharge summary.[134] As recommended by the Society of Hospital Medicine's Quality and Patient Safety Committee, the checklist in an ideal discharge summary would include a list of pending tests and the responsible person to whom the results should be sent.135 One study (of approximately 700 patients in two medical facilities) found large deficiencies in documenting tests with pending results as well as including information on the follow-up provider.136 With appropriate documentation of patient information, providers outside of the hospital setting have access to timely information regarding the patient's condition, prior treatment history, medication usage, and laboratory test results, among others.

Improving Patient-Provider Communication

A number of factors may influence the ability of the patient or the caregiver to appropriately manage the patient's condition or illness. Ineffective communication between physicians or other hospital staff and their patients has been identified as a factor leading to lack of prescribed medication compliance.[137] First, a patient may not sufficiently understand his or her condition. For example, written discharge information may be given to patients with limited literacy or English proficiency; alternatively, these instructions may conflict with a patient's cultural values. Other contributing factors may include cognitive impairment and lack of access to services. The range and complexity of choices that patients confront—including whether and when to seek care, how to reconcile conflicting opinions from various providers or family members, and the introduction of technology into everyday decisions—may make patient engagement challenging.[138]

Transitional care teams have emphasized educating patients about warning signs or "red flags" indicating deterioration in the patient's health condition.[139]

Coaching has been used, with the intent to "activate" patients, in an effort to make them better advocates for their own care, to teach patients and their caregivers the steps to take in the event of an emergency, and to improve patients' ability to communicate with other providers they encounter. "Activation" itself—an emerging topic of study in health services research—has been associated with better quality of care.[140] However, adequate patient follow-up can also be also dependent on the availability of patient resources, such as housing and the presence of informal caregivers, factors that are outside the control of the hospital.[141]

In addition, studies suggest that post-discharge contact with patients by hospital personnel or transitional care staff can address patient-provider communication gaps and patient compliance issues. There has been mixed evidence from the substantial amount of research evaluating the benefit of post-discharge telephone calls, either as one part of a transitional care program or as a separate intervention. [142] However, certain proponents support the implementation of a post-discharge phone call program to reinforce discharge instructions, medication changes and follow-up care plans as well as to monitor clinical developments of these patients and to intervene if necessary. Given the resources necessary for the program, targeting high risk patients may be warranted. [143]

Targeting Patients at Risk of Readmission

Generally, determining which readmissions are appropriate or which readmissions may be preventable involves a complex set of questions that are subject to intense debate among hospital advocates, researchers and policy makers. Academics have developed predictive models to identify which patient populations are at greatest risk for hospitalizations and rehospitalizations.[144] However, these clinical models used to predict readmission risk have limited success with such predictions.[145] Alternatively, hospitals can identify patients who have a high risk of readmissions and are appropriate candidates for intervention, such as those with a history of a recent admission or readmission, those with longer-than-expected stays or high-risk diagnoses and those with diabetes.

As currently structured, the HRRP program provides some incentive for hospitals to focus on managing the readmissions for Medicare patients initially admitted with one of the three applicable conditions, (at least until additional measures can be adopted in FY2015). Alternatively, hospitals may see attempts to target efforts to select patient populations as more costly than implementing systemic procedural and programmatic changes to address readmissions, particularly if the HRRP program is seen as likely to expand to other conditions or if other insurers are apt to become concerned with readmissions. As noted previously in *Table 2,* transitional care interventions frequently target patients with certain characteristics and individual circumstances, so hospitals could focus on managing the readmissions of the patients best situated to stay out of the hospital for 30 days. Simply, the response of any given hospital is difficult to predict in the abstract.

Accessing and Training Available Caregivers

Caregivers—family and friends who provide care generally without compensation— can play a significant role in the hospital discharge as well as post-discharge activities of Medicare beneficiaries. The ability of Medicare beneficiaries to perform activities of daily living, and also to make doctor's appointments and handle financial transactions may be compromised as they age or suffer from cognitive impairments. [146] Those patients who have access to caregiver support may be at less risk for a hospital readmission than patients who live alone and have restricted access to caregivers.[147,148] Caregivers and patients may work together to address the patient's primary needs—medication management, management of the patient's condition, and the patient's confidence in knowing how to care for himself or herself following the hospital discharge.[149] A number of the transitional care models emphasize inclusion of the caregiver during "coaching" sessions with patients in the hospital prior to discharge as well as during follow-up after the discharge. This training of caregivers can enhance the quality of the assistance that they provide to patients and hence could minimize readmissions. Of course, a hospital has no control over whether a patient has access to an engaged caregiver. The hospital's goal would be to enable any available caregiver to give the strongest possible support to the discharged patient.

Minimizing Medical Errors

There is evidence that avoidable medical errors occur in the inpatient hospital setting and that these errors can cause adverse events resulting in readmissions for some Medicare beneficiaries.[150] Medical errors, which may result in ineffective or incorrect treatments as well as preventable injuries or death, include

- errors related to diagnosis or treatment;
- medication errors, such as prescribing, modification, and administration of medications to patients; and
- surgical errors, which are mistakes or omissions made during and around the performance of surgical procedures (such as wound infections, deterioration of a clinical condition, postoperative complications).

One study found that, of patients undergoing a major surgery, those who experience a postsurgical adverse event are at substantially higher risk (one-third higher) of a hospital readmission than patients not experiencing such an adverse event.[151] Although it is unlikely that all medical and surgical errors that result in readmissions could be eliminated, additional efforts might be made to minimize such errors and their implications. Options may include the implementation of systemwide quality improvements in hospitals, such as the establishment of new medical and surgical protocols (and checklists related to those protocols), payment incentives to providers for additional quality improvements or penalties for the lack of such improvements, and the addition of new training requirements for hospital staff, among others.

Arranging for Post-Discharge Care

Medicare COP requires a hospital (1) to develop any necessary discharge plan and arrange for its initial implementation; (2) to counsel the patient, family members or interested parties as necessary to prepare them for post-hospital care and advise them of its availability; and (3) to transfer or refer patients along with necessary medical information to appropriate facilities, agencies, or outpatient services as needed for follow-up or ancillary care. In the view of CMS, "hospitals can communicate effectively with post-acute providers and take other measures that can better prepare a patient for discharge to reduce the risk of readmission."[152] Half of Medicare patients with a medical condition who were readmitted within 30 after discharge did not have an outpatient physician claim submitted within that time period.[153] Transitional care teams or others within hospitals may be able to assist patients by scheduling appointments for the patient following the hospital discharge or communicating with the outpatient provider. As mentioned earlier, these teams may also ensure that the providers in the outpatient setting have access to a complete and detailed history of the patient's treatment, medications, and other information.

Care teams in the hospital can also collect provider contact information and create useful resource compendiums for patients. For instance, under the Project RED program, the discharge advocate creates an after-hospital care plan with provider contact information, a calendar with appointment and test dates, a medication schedule, and other resources intended to be user-friendly.[154] As discussed earlier in this report, other transitional care programs have similar tools designed to assist patients with post-discharge care.[155] Several of these programs last four weeks or longer and include telephone or in-person contact with the patient, such as visiting the patient's home or accompanying the patient to a skilled nursing facility or outpatient provider. In one of the care models, the "coach" communicates with the outpatient provider following the first patient visit subsequent to hospital discharge.[156] Again, the extent to which a hospital decides to adopt these interventions and the benefit to a particular patient will vary.

Developing Collaborations between Providers and Community Organizations

Hospital readmissions may be associated with problems that are beyond the "four walls" of the hospital or other institutions that treat patients. To improve transitions in care and, perhaps, reduce readmissions, providers must collaborate across organizational and service-line boundaries and enlist the resources of community organizations to provide complementary services. Readmissions can reflect care provided by hospitals but also by outpatient physicians and post-acute providers, as well as supportive services to seniors or disabled adults within the community. A number of programs target the health of those who can be at risk for readmissions. These can include programs run through local or state agencies, including Departments of Public Health.[157] However, such coordination is difficult because the different entities may not share information or have existing financial or referral relationships. Also, communities may have different infrastructures or practices when it comes to providing hospital or post-acute care. The supply of resources in particular communities may also affect health care utilization, including readmissions. [158,159] Researchers have found that collective action among community providers, including hospitals and other health care providers, can be useful in creating an efficient health care system; this in turn may result in lower readmission rates for hospitals in such communities.

To help hospitals reduce readmissions, QIOs and others have focused on bringing together providers and community organizations to build coalitions to understand common patient populations and their care deficiencies, and implement necessary improvements in the different health care settings.[160,161] One of the necessary steps towards understanding readmissions patterns will depend upon the ability to track patients across providers and systems. As noted by Jencks, individual hospitals need access to all-hospital (perhaps all-payer) data to track their readmissions since 20% to 40% of patients are rehospitalized in other facilities.[162] To that end, CMS is required to collect and report on the hospital readmissions for all patients.[163]

Appendix B. Different Readmission Measures and Methodologies

Generally speaking, a hospital readmission is an admission to a hospital within a certain time frame, following an original admission and discharge. A readmission rate is the number of rehospitalizations (numerator) divided by the number of index (or initial) discharges (denominator) in a given period of time. However, different definitions of the "number" of readmissions and the definition of the "number" of discharges, result in a wide divergence of readmission measures. For example, a readmission measure is dependent on the definitions of the universe of patients who are included as part of the measure, what types of cases are excluded as index admissions, what types of cases are excluded as countable rehospitalizations, the risk-adjustment methodology used to adjust the numerator and/or denominator, how multiple readmissions for the same patient are counted, whether to consider only clinically related admissions, and whether to distinguish and exclude planned surgical, planned medical or other readmissions. Not only can these technical decisions result in different readmission rates, but also in different hospital performance rankings with respect to those relative readmission rates.

Although several entities have worked to identify preventable readmissions, there is no consensus on the method to distinguish readmissions that might be avoided from those that are unavoidable. Different approaches result in different potentially preventable readmission (PPR) rates. Answers to these questions may help to define PPRs:

- Does a clinical relationship exist between the admission and a readmission?
- Which conditions or procedures should be counted as potentially preventable and which should not be counted as such (e.g., malignant cancers)? and,
- Should readmissions to a different acute-care hospital be added to the count of readmissions for the hospital with the initial admission?

This appendix will discuss five approaches to determining readmission measures: (1) the Jencks framework which categorizes readmissions as planned and unplanned and then potentially preventable or not; (2) the warranty provided by the Geisinger Health System that covers specified adverse events and/or readmissions resulting from a particular surgery and (3) the all-cause measure used by UnitedHealthcare (a health care insurer) which defines PPR more narrowly than Jencks; (4) the 3M approach which defines certain preventable readmissions as readmissions related to selected medical conditions; and (5) the NQF all-cause readmission calculation adopted by CMS, which generally does not account for the relationship between the index discharge and the readmission.

The Jencks Readmission Framework

Dr. Stephen Jencks used the following framework to discuss which cases might be identified as PPRs in a presentation before the National Medicare Readmissions Summit in Washington, DC in June 2009. [164] In general, unplanned readmissions within 30 days constitute 90% of all 30-day readmissions. Reducing these readmissions could reduce Medicare expenditures. *Table B-1* provides four categories of readmissions, depending on whether or not they are related and/or planned.

- *Related and Unplanned.* Some readmissions can be considered both related to the initial admission and unplanned. For instance, a person may be readmitted to a hospital to address an adverse event caused by an infection or sepsis, which resulted from problems occurring during a surgery. Another example is a person with heart failure who is readmitted for chest pain.

- *Related and Planned.* Other readmissions are those that are related to the initial hospitalization and are scheduled in advance by a hospital in order to deliver follow-up medical care, perform medical procedures, or both. For example, a patient may be admitted for heart failure and readmitted later for the placement of a cardiac stent.[165] Such readmissions are often part of the treatment plan for certain conditions.
- *Unrelated and Planned.* Still other readmissions are those that are unrelated and planned. For example, an admission for chronic obstructive pulmonary disorder (COPD)[166] could be followed by a readmission for a scheduled hip replacement surgery.
- *Unrelated and Unplanned.* Finally, some readmissions are unrelated to the initial hospitalization and are also unplanned. For example, readmissions for burns or traumas that are caused by accidents can be both unrelated and unplanned. Another example might be an initial admission for a gastrointestinal disorder followed by a readmission for skin cancer.

Table B-1. Jencks Readmission Framework Four Kinds of Hospitalizations

Type	Examples
Related and Unplanned	Heart failure, pneumonia, stroke
Related and Planned	Chemotherapy, staged surgery
Unrelated and planned	Unrelated procedures
Unrelated and unplanned	Some kinds of trauma and harm from the environment

Source: Stephen F. Jencks, M.D., M.P.H., "Rehospitalization: Understanding the Challenge," Presentation at the National Medicare Readmissions Summit, Washington, DC, June 1, 2009.

Note: In his analysis, Jencks excluded patients who were transferred on the day of discharge to other acute care hospitals, including patients admitted to hospital specialty units, inpatient rehabilitation facilities, and long-term care hospitals, and patients rehospitalized for rehabilitation.

Geisinger and UnitedHealthcare Group (UHG) Approaches

Payers, providers, hospitals, and health systems have defined PPRs in different ways. The Geisinger Health System and UHG, for example, are two entities that have tried to define PPRs for the purpose of implementing strategies to reduce hospital readmissions rates. Under the Geisinger ProvenCare program, preoperative, inpatient and postoperative care within 90 days for nonemergency coronary artery bypass graft (CABG) surgery is covered by one fixed price;[167] Geisinger physicians performing these CABGs on patients covered by the Geisinger Health Plan agreed not to be paid for readmissions within 90 days that were "not unrelated" to the initial surgery. Examples of such readmissions include atrial fibrillation; venous thrombosis; infections due to an internal prosthetic device, implant, or graft; and postoperative infections. By using this approach to defining readmissions, Geisinger avoids having to finely distinguish between readmissions that are *clearly* related and those that are *possibly* related to the surgery.[168]

In its reporting of readmission rates for California hospitals, UHG uses a different approach. As discussed by MedPAC, only readmissions that are billed under the same Medicare payment diagnostic category (MS-DRG),[169] or those that are for infections, are considered reasonably preventable. For example, if the initial hospitalization and a readmission both were coded as MSDRG-313 (chest pain), the readmission would be considered reasonably preventable. Conversely, if the initial hospitalization was coded as MS-DRG 304 (hypertension with major complications/comorbidities) and the readmission was coded as MS-DRG 313, the readmission would not be considered reasonably preventable.[170] To adjust for patient risk severity, the UHG approach compares each patient with all other patients statewide with the same initial DRG.[171]

3M's PPR Approach

MedPAC examined the issue of hospital readmissions and its implications for the Medicare program using 3M's proprietary software.[172] Broadly speaking, in the 3M PPR approach, readmissions for a medical condition that follow an initial medical or surgical admission are likely to be considered preventable, whereas surgical readmissions are not likely to be preventable.[173] A medical readmission would include, among others, heart failure, pneumonia, and chronic obstructive pulmonary disease (COPD), and a surgical readmission would include, among others, cardiac stent placement, major hip or knee surgery, and vascular surgery. Under this definition, however, unintended results might occur. For example, a patient who is admitted with a heart attack and then readmitted to the hospital for diabetes would be considered a PPR.[174] On the other hand, readmission for an appendectomy following an admission for pneumonia would not considered preventable.[175]

All Patient Refined Diagnosis Related Groups (APR-DRGs) are used to classify patients according to their reason for admission and to establish the existence of a clinical relationship between an initial admission and a readmission.[176] APR-DRGs are also stratified according to the patient's severity of illness (SOI) level, which is based upon secondary patient diagnoses.

The 3M approach aims to refine the definition of preventable readmission and to ensure that the readmission is clinically related to the initial admission by using expert panels. The experts assess whether or not there was a reasonable expectation that the readmission could have been prevented by (1) provision of quality of care in the hospital; (2) adequate discharge planning; (3) adequate post-discharge follow-up; and/or (4) improved coordination between hospitals and providers outside of the hospital setting. For the purposes of this definition, exclusions include major or metastatic malignancies, multiple trauma, burns, certain chronic conditions (such as cystic fibrosis that are seen as not preventable or are expected to require follow-up care) and neonatal and obstetrical admissions. The analysis also excludes patients who left the hospital against medical advice.[177]

The algorithm created by 3M identifies readmissions within 7 to 30 days following the index hospital admission, depending upon the length of stay parameters specified by the user. A readmission chain includes the initial admission and any subsequent readmissions determined to be related to the initial admission. Under the 3M approach, an adjusted PPR rate is calculated using the number of readmission chains as the numerator, rather than the total number of PPRs.[178] The denominator consists of all candidate admissions defined as those admissions that could have been linked to a PPR. APR-DRGs and SOI levels, as well as age and the presence or absence of mental health or substance abuse comorbidities, are then used to create a hospital's expected number of PPRs. Finally, the hospital's adjusted PPR rate is calculated by dividing a hospital's actual number of PPRs by the hospital's risk-adjusted expected number of PPRs.

CMS addressed the use of the 3M PPR approach for HRRP in the FY2012 final rule in response to a public comment. Although Florida uses the 3M PPR measure, after review by NQF in 2009, the measure was not endorsed. According to CMS, the NQF steering committee expressed concerns about the reliability of the methodology used to specify 98,000 admission-readmission pairs (such as an HF admission followed by a readmission for a fall) as either clinically related (and therefore preventable) or not related (and not preventable). The NQF Steering Committee did not think those judgments were reliable and rejected the measure in part on this issue. CMS agreed that a measure cannot accurately determine what is related and not related simply on the basis of the coded diagnosis for the admission and readmission.[179]

CMS' All-Cause Readmission Measure

As noted earlier, CMS adopted the NQF-endorsed, risk-standardized 30-day readmission measures which is currently publically reported on the Hospital Compare website as part of their FY2012 rulemaking process.[180] The methodology calculates an all-cause readmission measure using administrative claims data for Medicare FFS beneficiaries who are age 65 and over for three conditions (HF, PN and AMI). In 2015, this will be expanded to seven conditions. Only one readmission during the 30 days following the discharge from the initial hospitalization will count as a readmission.[181] A subsequent admission to a different hospital is counted as a readmission for the hospital in which the original, index admission took place.[182]

Section 1886(q)(5)(A) of the SSA establishes that the measures should exclude readmissions that are unrelated to the index admission (such as a planned readmission or a transfer to another acute hospital). However, only the AMI 30-day risk-standardized readmission measure excludes certain planned follow-up procedures when counting readmissions.[183] The AMI measure also excludes patients who are discharged alive on the same day of admission.[184] Other types of patient events are excluded from all three measures: patients who die during the initial hospitalization, same day readmissions to the same hospital for the same condition, patients who are transferred out of the hospital to another acute care facility, and patients who are discharged against medical advice.[185]

In the view of CMS, many cases with seemingly unrelated diagnoses may correspond to the patient diagnosis during the original hospitalization and therefore determining whether the readmission is related to the original admission cannot be made solely on the basis of the admitting diagnosis for the readmission.[186] Also, in their view, rehospitalizations that are unrelated to the original admission should not affect some hospitals disproportionately, because similarly situated patients should have the same probability of readmission, regardless of where the initial hospitalization occurred. Finally, the exclusions of transfers to other applicable hospitals is seen as sufficient to meet the requirement that certain unrelated readmissions be excluded from the measures.

Hospital advocates maintain that the small set of existing exclusions does not meet the statutory requirement that unrelated readmissions not be counted; in their view, without additional exclusions from the existing measures, hospitals will be penalized for readmissions beyond their control.[187] To that end, hospital advocates suggest that CMS conduct a study to determine the common reasons for readmissions and identify unrelated readmissions. In the meantime, these advocates recommend that patients with certain conditions (such as cancer, trauma, burns, substance abuse or psychiatric disorders) be excluded; that a claims modifier be implemented so a hospital can identify planned readmissions; and that other existing classification schemes (discussed above) be used to identify related readmissions.[188] CMS declined to make such exclusions in its FY2012 rulemaking because they viewed this action as inconsistent with the statutory requirement that CMS adopt the measures as endorsed by NQF. CMS stated that additional readmissions seen as properly excluded from the existing readmission measures would be brought to NQF for review and potential endorsement. Any revised and endorsed measure would be subsequently included in future rulemaking actions.[189]

As endorsed by NQF, Medicare's time frame for a readmission is 30 days.[190] For the FY2013 hospital readmission analysis, CMS will assess hospital performance on readmissions using a three-year measurement period (the applicable period) starting in July 1, 2008 through June 30, 2011. While the 30-day readmission time frame did not raise industry concerns, the use of a three-year performance period beginning before ACA's enactment date (as well as the 25 minimum case threshold) did generate public comments. Although CMS finalized its proposal to use 25 cases and a three-year data set, it is conducting an analysis to determine if a different sample size or a shorter time period can yield reliable data.[191]

The risk-standardization method is designed to adjust for the unique mix of patients that each hospital treated during the study period, including patients' past medical history (for the past 12 months) and patients' comorbid conditions.[192] The hierarchical logistic regression used by CMS also adjusts for the patient's age, gender, and a hospital-specific quality component.[193] The measures do not adjust for a patient's admission source and discharge disposition, because these factors are associated with the structure of the health care system and not patient clinical risk factors.[194] The model does not account for patient socioeconomic status (SES) either.[195] As noted in the measures report, the association between SES status and health outcomes can be due, in part, to differences in the quality of health care provided to patients; thus, including SES in the risk adjustment may suggest that hospitals that treat lower SES patients are held to different readmission standards than those hospitals treating higher SES patients. [196]

This risk adjustment methodology attracted significant public comment during the FY2012 rulemaking process. As noted by CMS, many commenters argued that the measures should be adjusted for patient characteristics beyond medical diagnosis, age, and gender which are currently included in the risk adjustment methodology. Commenters believed that the methodology should include risk adjustment for patient race, language/English proficiency, life circumstances, environmental factors and that SES should be included in the methodology because of the potential impact of these factors on health outcomes. Omission of these factors, according to those commenters, may disproportionately affect hospitals serving a large number of minorities and ultimately adversely affect the quality of and access to care for minorities. CMS did not agree that the NQF-endorsed risk adjustment methodology used in the HRRP would harm minorities. In the view of CMS, the current methodology adjusts for case-mix differences based on the clinical status of the patient at the time of admission to the hospital and would account for the extent that race or SES would influence the disease burden in certain patient groups. Also, these adjustments are not seen as appropriate by CMS because the association between these factors and health outcomes can be due, in part, to differences in the quality of care received by these groups of patients that should not be obscured. As CMS noted, risk-adjusting for patient race, for instance, may suggest that hospitals with a high proportion of minority patients are held to different standards of quality than hospitals treating fewer minority patients.[197]

As directed by statute, the risk-standardized readmission ratio is calculated as the number of adjusted actual or predicted readmissions divided by the number of expected readmissions at a given hospital. [198] The ratio is measure of relative performance: if a hospital performs better than the average hospital that admitted similar patients (in terms of the measured risk factors for the included demographic characteristics and comorbidities), the ratio will be less than one. Those hospitals performing worse than the average hospital, after risk adjustment, will have a ratio greater than one. As finalized by CMS, the

NQF-endorsed measures calculated the risk- standardized ratio using hierarchical logistic regression modeling to account for each hospital's unique quality of care for its patient population and which produces a predicted over expected ratio.

Finally, several criticisms have been raised about the hierarchical model used in CMS measure development. The shrinkage affect reduces the variation of hospital performance which can obscure differences in provider performance and render the information not as useful to consumers. [199] Also, the model masks the performance of small hospitals, because these entities get a rate close to the national mean. As noted by MedPAC, the smaller the hospital, the less of its information is used and the more of the national average is used. In their view, this method will tend to underestimate excess readmissions, especially for small hospitals with high readmission rates. Moreover, this methodology is also difficult to explain to the public and other stakeholders who are more familiar with the results of a methodology that uses an observed over expected ratio determined in a logistic regression model.[200]

As discussed in the next section, depending upon the methodology used—such as what is included in the numerator and denominator, the time period used, and the choice of the statistical model--readmission rates can vary considerably.[201]

Measure Design Can Affect Hospitals' Readmission Rates

Using Massachusetts hospital discharge data, Boutwell and Jencks measured the statewide 30-day readmission rates (for medical conditions only) under three different methodologies. The 3M PPR readmission rate was 10.7%; the UHG readmission rate was 19.3%; and CMS all-cause readmission rate was 21.9%. Individual hospital performance rankings (by readmission rate) also varied significantly; a hospital that ranked first with the CMS methodology was ranked ninth with the 3M PPR methodology and ranked forty-third with the UHG methodology.

Finally, the time interval or the period of time between the date of initial discharge and the date of readmission will also affect readmission measures. CMS (and NQF) have adopted 30 days as the readmission period, but readmissions have also been established within 7, 15, or 30 days following discharge from the initial hospital stay. For some purposes, the time frame can also be defined as the period up to 2, 3, 4, or 12 months following discharge. Simply, the use of longer time frames when establishing readmission rates could result in larger savings for Medicare. MedPAC states that annual Medicare spending on PPRs is $5 billion for 7-day, $8 billion for 15- day, and $12 billion for 30-day readmissions.[202] Yet, such longer time frames raise challenges for identifying whether a readmission is related to an initial admission and if so, which entities would be held responsible for avoiding the rehospitalization.

Appendix C. Illustrative Example of the Hospital Readmission Reduction Program Calculation

This appendix provides an illustrative example for CMS's Hospital Readmission Reduction Program (HRRP) calculation. A full description of HRRP is provided previously in the report. This appendix describes each of the components of the formula, followed by a hypothetical example of how that formula will be applied in practice.

Each component of the formula is described in statute as follows:

- Determine the excess readmissions ratio for the hospital defined as the risk-adjusted *predicted* readmissions divided by the risk-adjusted *expected* readmissions;
- Determine the aggregate payments for excess readmissions for the hospital defined as the product of three components:
  - The base operating DRG payments for the applicable conditions,
  - The number of admissions for those conditions, and
  - The hospital's excess readmissions ratio;
- Determine the aggregate payment for all discharges for the hospital defined as the sum of base operating DRG payments for all discharges for all conditions in the hospital;
- Determine the excess readmissions payment ratio defined as 1 minus the ratio of the aggregate payments for excess readmissions for the hospital to the aggregate payments for all discharges -- which can be displayed as:

$$1-\left(\frac{\text{Aggregate payments for all excess readmission}}{\text{Aggregate payments for all discharges}}\right)$$

- Determine the adjustment factor by using greater of the excess readmissions payment ratio or the floor adjustment factor (of 0.99 of the discharge payments in FY2013, 0.98 of the discharge in FY2014, 0.97 in FY2015 and in subsequent fiscal years (effectively limiting the adjustment to no more than a 1% reduction in FY 2013, 2% in FY 2014 and 3% thereafter);
- Determine the adjustment to the hospital payments for excess readmissions by multiplying the base operating DRG payment amount for discharges from the hospital by the applicable adjustment factor.

To summarize, to calculate the penalty, the amount of excess payments made for each applicable condition is determined as the product of the number of patients with that condition, the base DRG payment for those patients and the percentage of readmissions above the expected readmissions for that hospital. That calculation is done for each of the applicable conditions. These excessive payments are summed and then divided by the hospital's total operating base payments for Medicare to derive a penalty percentage. However, that penalty is capped, depending upon the year.

The application of the formula is best understood through an illustrative example for FY2013 which may not represent the final calculation as implemented by CMS. Consider the situation of hospital A with 260 initial admissions for the applicable conditions and 3,250 total Medicare discharges.

In this example, the hospital's excess payment ratio is not the adjustment factor used to calculate its readmission penalty, because that reduction of 2% is larger than would be permitted according to statute. Instead in FY2013, the floor of 0.99 (or a 1% reduction) would be applied to the hospital's base operating payment per discharge used to reimburse that hospital for all Medicare discharges in that fiscal year.

As noted by CMS, some commenters believe that the penalty should only be applied to readmissions for the applicable conditions and not to all the hospital's Medicare discharges.

Others have stated the readmission payment penalty should be applied to the number of excessive number of readmissions for the applicable conditions, instead of a penalty on all Medicare discharges. Certain hospital advocates have stated that the excess readmissions ratio was incorrectly established in statute and the existing formula will result in penalties far greater than Medicare's payments for excess readmissions.

Table C-1.Illustrative Calculation of Hospital HRRP Penalty

	Steps in Calculation	Column B
1	Initial Admissions for Applicable Condition	260
2	Risk-adjusted Predicted Number of Readmissions	50
3	Risk-adjusted Expected Number of Readmissions	40
4	Excess Readmissions Ratio [B2/B3]	1.25
5	*DISCHARGES*	
6	Total Medicare Discharges for Applicable Conditions	310
7	Total Medicare Discharges for All Conditions	3,250
8	BASE OPERATING PAYMENTS	
9	Base Operating Payments Per Discharge	$7,150
10	*CALCULATION OF RATIO ADJUSTMENT FACTOR*	
11	Aggregate Payments for Excess Readmissions [B9*B6*(B4-1)]	$554,125
12	Aggregate Payments for All Medicare Discharges [B9*B7]	$23,237,500
13	Excess Readmissions Payment Ratio [1-(B11/B12)]	0.98
14	FY2013 Floor Adjustment Factor	0.99
15	*CALCULATION OF READMISSION PENALTY*	
16	Adjusted Base Operating Payments Per Discharge [B9*0.99]	$7,079
17	Total Hospital Payments With Readmission Penalty [B16*B7]	$23,005,125
18	Total Hospital Payments Absent Readmission Penalty [B9*B7]	$23,237,500
19	Readmission Penalty in FY2013 [B18-B17 or .01*B18]	$232,375

Source: CRS calculation.

Accordingly, they argued Congress should redefine the excess readmissions ratio as the percentage of Medicare excess readmissions to total Medicare admissions (not as a ratio of predicted to expected admissions); at a minimum, with the readmission penalty capped at the amount of actual Medicare payments for excess readmissions.[203] MedPAC has indicated that the formula in the law produces a higher count of excess readmissions than if the calculation were based on the difference between the actual and expected readmissions and will produce a higher estimate of Medicare spending on readmissions. This tendency is offset by the hierarchical models used to establish the readmission measures which blend the experience of the hospital with the average experience in the country. In MedPAC's view, any reexamination of the readmission policy should consider both of these aspects.[204]

However, if the penalties are designed to motivate hospitals to work to minimize readmissions, there is some question whether smaller penalties will provide sufficient incentives to hospitals to dedicate adequate resources to address systemic hospital processes affecting readmissions. Some believe that the existing HRRP penalty may not provide adequate incentives for hospitals to address readmissions and suggest that it should be restructured. [205] Hospitals with lower than average readmission rates for all three conditions face no financial penalty. Hospitals facing penalties may be better off financially if they maintain the status quo, given the costs of implementing transition care interventions and the lost revenue from readmissions. These issues and others associated with the HRRP payment adjustment are likely to garner significant attention over the upcoming IPPS rulemaking cycle.

End Notes

[1] Bernard Friedman and Jayasree Basu, "The Rate and Cost of Hospital Readmissions for Preventable Conditions," Medical Care Research and Review, vol. 61, no. 2 (June 2004), pp. 225-240.

[2] MedPAC, Report to Congress: Promoting Greater Efficiency in Medicare, June 2007, Chapter 5. See http://www.medpac.gov/documents/Jun07_EntireReport.pdf. (Subsequently referred to as MedPAC, Greater Efficiency, June 2007).

[3] Although this report focuses on readmissions, some of these same strategies are thought to address preventable initial admissions. In fact, hospitals with high admission rates may be most likely to have high readmission rates, suggesting that addressing the needs of those patients most likely to be admitted may also reduce overall readmission rates. Arnold M. Epstein, Ashish K.Jha, and John E Orav, "The Relationship Between Hospital Admission Rates and Rehospitalizations." New England Journal of Medicine (NEJM); vol. 365 (December 15, 2011), pp. 2287-2295. (Subsequently referred to as Epstein et al., "The Relationship Between Hospital Admission Rates and Rehospitalizations.")

[4] New Jersey (21.9%), Louisiana (21.9%), and Illinois (21.7%) had the highest while Oregon (15.7%), Utah (14.2%), and Idaho (13.3%) had the lowest readmission rates for Medicare beneficiaries. Stephen F. Jencks, Mark V. Williams, and Eric A. Coleman, "Rehospitalizations among Patients in the Medicare Fee-for-Service Program," New England Journal of Medicine, vol. 360 (April 2, 2009), pp. 1418-1428. (Subsequently referred to as Jencks, Williams, and Coleman, "FFS Medicare Rehospitalizations." NEJM, vol. 360 pp. 1418-1428) Also see as Epstein, et al, "The Relationship Between Hospital Admission Rates and Rehospitalizations."

[5] MedPAC, Report to Congress: Regional Variation in Medicare Service Use, January, 2011. See http://www.medpac.gov/documents/Jan11_RegionalVariation_report.pdf.

[6] David Goodman, Elliot Fisher, and Chiang-Hua Chang, After Hospitalization: A Dartmouth Atlas Report on Post-Acute Care for Medicare Beneficiaries, September 28, 2011. Available at: http://www.dartmouthatlas.org/data/topic/ topic.aspx?cat=30.

[7] Factors such as differences in patient status, the quality of inpatient care, and the availability of ambulatory services in the community may also contribute to differences in readmission rates across certain regions and hospitals. Ibid, p. 6.

[8] The policy factors affecting these rehospitalizations may depend upon whether the beneficiary was originally admitted from his or her home or a nursing home. Vincent Mor, Orna Intrator, Zhanlian Feng,and David C. Grabowski, "The Revolving Door of

Rehospitalizations from Skilled Nursing Facilities," Health Affairs, vol, 29, no 1, January 2010, pp. 57-64.

[9] Rehospitalization rates vary by type of SNF and ownership as well as the percent of dual-eligible beneficiaries treated in the facilities. MedPAC, Report to Congress: Medicare Payment Policy March 2012, Chapter 7. pp. 194-200. http://www.medpac.gov/chapters/Mar12_Ch07.pdf.

[10] As an added complication, each post-acute provider, including SNFs, inpatient rehabilitation facilities (IRFs), longterm care hospitals (LTCHs) and home health agencies (HHAs) has a different Medicare prospective payment system, patient assessment instrument (if any), and Medicare coverage requirement.

[11] Transitional care complements but has different features than other care management models, such as care coordination, disease management and case management. Mary D. Naylor, Linda Aiken, Ellen Kurtzman, Danielle Olds, and Karen Hirshman, "THE CARE SPAN: The Importance of Transitional Care In Achieving Health Reform," Health Affairs, vol 30, no. 4 (April 2011) pp. 746-754. (Subsequently, Naylor et al, "The Importance of Transitional Care").

[12] One study reports that (1) the cost of copayments for medications and follow-up visits, (2) lack of home health coverage if the beneficiary does not meet Medicare's current home-bound requirements, and, (3) lack of payment for transitional care services (post-discharge phone calls, coaching services, and clinical services) are factors that providers see as barriers to their efforts to reduce rehospitalizations. Amy Boutwell, Marian Johnson, Patricia Rutherford, et al., "An Early Look at A Four-State Initiative to Reduce Avoidable Hospital Readmissions," Health Affairs, vol 30, no. 7 (July 2011) pp. 1272-1280.

[13] Certain changes to the QIO program were included as part of the Trade Adjustment Assistance Extension Act of 2011 (P.L. 112-40) that was enacted on October 21, 2011. These changes apply to QIO contracts entered into or renewed starting January 1, 2012. The QIO's 10th SOW which established projects to address hospital readmissions is not affected.

[14] Although outside of the scope of this discussion, other initiatives within the Department of Health and Human Services (HHS) also seek to reduce hospital readmissions and warrant mentioning, in passing. For instance, the Partnership for Patients: Better Care, Lower Costs is a public-private partnership that as one of its goals seeks to reduce hospital readmissions by 20% over a three-year period. Other information technology (IT) initiatives within HHS seek to improve care transitions for discharged patients, particularly the first two projects announced under the Investing in Innovation (i2) Initiative within the Office of the National Coordinator for Health Information Technology (ONC). The first project sought (and found three) developers to create a web-based application of the CMS discharge checklist to help patients and their caregivers leave the hospital. At the end of January, 2012, ONC announced a second IT project, the discharge follow-up challenge to assist with scheduling of post-hospital appointments and testing. Although not specifically targeted to Medicare beneficiaries, these efforts, if successful, are likely to impact Medicare's readmissions as well.

[15] Medicare shared savings programs, including Accountable Care Organizations (ACOs) and other demonstration programs concerned with case management or medical monitoring programs for chronically ill beneficiaries, are outside the scope of this discussion.

[16] 84.4% of the rehospitalizations after an initial admission for a medical condition and 72.2% of the rehospitalizations after an initial admission for a surgical condition were for a medical diagnosis. Jencks, Williams, and Coleman, "Feefor-Service Medicare Rehospitalizations," NEJM, vol 360. pp. 1418-1428.

[17] In a meta-analysis of 44 studies, the mean readmission rate was 34% for patients with chronic illnesses compared to a mean, overall rate of 27%. Karen L. Soeken, Patricia A. Prescott, and Dorothy G. Herron, et al., "Predictors of Hospital Readmission: A Meta-Analysis," Evaluation and the Health Professions, vol. 14, no. 3 (1991), pp. 262-281.

[18] Among those 65 years and older, patients with five or more medically comorbid conditions had odds that were more than 2.5 times the odds of patients without those conditions to have an unplanned readmission within 30 days. Edward. R. Marcantonio, Sylvia McKean, Michael Goldfinger, Sharon Kleefield, Mark Yurkofsky, Troyen A. Brennan, "Factors Associated with Unplanned Hospital Readmission Among Patients 65 years of Age and Older in a Medicare Managed Care Plan," The American Journal of Medicine, vol. 107, no. 1 (July 1999), pp. 13-17.

[19] 2005 data indicate that 30-day readmission rates for patients with end-stage renal disease are nearly twice as high as readmission rates for patients without end-stage renal disease. MedPAC, Greater Efficiency, June 2007, p. 107.

[20] Jencks, Williams, and Coleman, "FFS Medicare Rehospitalizations." NEJM, vol. 360 pp. 1418-1428. Presentation by Stephen F. Jencks, at the National Hospital Payment Reform Summit, Washington, DC, September 17, 2009.

[21] This trend was demonstrated using Medicare data for FFS beneficiaries discharged from acute care hospitals from 1997, 2002, and 2007. These differences may be attributable to patients with high clinical severity scores having increased, unobserved clinical severity or not receiving high-quality transitional care services. Matthew Press, Amol Navathe, Jingsan Zhu, Wei Chen, Jessica Mittler, Dennis Scanlon, and Kevin Volpp, "Clinical Severity in the Measurement of Readmission Rates: A Comparison of Medicare Beneficiaries in 1997 and 2007." Paper presented at the 2011 Academy Health Annual Research Meeting, Seattle, WA.

[22] Devan Kansagara, Honora Englander, and Amanda Salanitro, et al., "Risk Prediction Models for Hospital Readmission: A Systematic Review," JAMA, vol. 306, no. 15 (October 19, 2011), pp. 1688-1698.

[23] Joshua West, Larry Gamm, and Brock Oxford, et al., "Determinants of Preventable Readmissions in the United States: A Systematic Review," Implementation Science, vol. 5, no. 88 (2010), pp. 1-28.

[24] Joseph S. Ross, Gregory K. Mulvey, and Brett Stauffer, et al., "Statistical Models and Patient Predictors of Readmission for Heart Failure," Archives of Internal Medicine, vol. 168, no. 13 (July 14, 2008), pp. 1371-1386.

[25] Karen E. Joynt and Ashish K. Jha, "Who Has Higher Readmission Rates for Heart Failure and Why: Implications for Efforts to Improve Care Using Financial Incentives," Circulation: Cardiovascular Quality and Outcomes. Journal of the American Heart Association, vol. 4 (June 2011), pp. 53-59.

[26] For instance, the odds of a readmission increases with age (per 10 years), as well as for females and African Americans (marginal increase in odds for this group), following coronary artery bypass graft surgery. Edward L. Hanna, Michael J. Racz, and Gary Walford, et al., "Predictors of Readmission for Complications of Coronary Artery Bypass Graft Surgery," JAMA, vol. 290, no. 6 (August 13, 2003), pp. 773-780.

[27] Trendwatch: Examining the Drivers of Readmissions and Reducing Unnecessary Readmissions for Better Patient Care, American Hospital Association, September 2011.

[28] This report will not use congestive heart failure (CHF) or heart failure (HF) interchangeably. In this instance, the study examined rates of CHF by race and site of care.

[29] Patients discharged from minority-serving hospitals had odds of readmission that were 1.23 times the odds of readmission for patients discharged from non-minority-serving hospitals. Black Medicare patients had odds of readmission that were 1.13 times the odds of readmission for white Medicare patients. These results varied by condition studied. Karen E. Joynt, E. John Orav, and Ashish K Jha, "Thirty-day Readmission Rates for Medicare Beneficiaries by Race and Site of Care," JAMA, vol. 305, no. 7, (February 16, 2011) pp. 675-681.

[30] See Harlan Krumholz, et al, "Standards for Statistical Models Used for Public Reporting of Health Outcomes, AHA Scientific Statement, Circulation: Cardiovascular Quality and Outcomes. Journal of the American Heart Association,: 2006: 113, pp. 456-462 for additional discussion with respect to preferred attributes of models used for publically reported outcome data. (Subsequently referred to as Krumholz et al, Standards for Statistical Models, AHA Scientific Statement Circulation: 2006).

[31] Mihai.Gheorghiade, and Eric D. Peterson, "Improving Postdischarge Outcomes in Patients Hospitalized for Acute Heart Failure Syndromes," JAMA, vol. 305, no. 23, (2011), pp. 2456-2457. (Subsequently referred to as Gheorghiade et al, "Improving Post Discharge Outcomes" JAMA vol. 305, no. 23, (2011), pp. 2456-2457).

[32] There was no bill for a visit to a physician's office between the patient's discharge and rehospitalization for more than half of the beneficiaries who were rehospitalized within 30 days after a medical discharge to the community. Jencks, Williams, and Coleman, "FFS Medicare Rehospitalizations." NEJM, vol. 360 p. 1426.

[33] Gheorghiade et al, "Improving Post Discharge Outcomes' JAMA vol. 305, no. 23, (2011), pp. 2456-2457.

[34] Robert L. Kane, "Finding The Right Level of Posthospital Care: 'We Didn't Realize There Was Any Other Option for Him," JAMA, vol 305, no. 3, (2010), pp. 284-293. This study also provides mixed evidence for whether certain post-discharge care settings (i.e., skilled nursing facilities or inpatient rehabilitation facilities) were better for specified patients (e.g., with strokes or hip fractures).

[35] Arnold M. Epstein, Ashish K Jha, and E. John Orav, (2011). "Explaining Variations in Readmission Rates: The Propensity to use Hospital Services." Paper presented at the 2011 AcademyHealth Annual Research Meeting, Seattle, WA.

[36] William Boulding, Seth Glickman, Matthew Manary, Kevin Schulman, and Richard Staelin, "Relationship Between Patient Satisfaction With Inpatient Care and Hospital Readmission Within 30 Days," The American Journal of Managed Care, vol. 17, (January 2011) no. 1, pp. 41-48.

[37] Vincent Mor and Richard W. Besdine,"Policy Options to Improve Discharge Planning and Reduce Rehospitalization," JAMA, vol. 305, no. 3, (January 19, 2011), pp. 302-303.

[38] Important information in this discussion is taken from the Care Transitions Quality Improvement Organization Support Center (QIOSC). This information may be accessed at http://www.cfmc.org/integratingcare/toolkit.htm.

[39] Lena M. Chen, Ashish K Jha, Stuart Guterman, Abigail B. Ridgway, E. John Orav, and Arnold M. Epstein, "Hospital Cost of Care, Quality of Care, and Readmission Rates: Penny Wise and Pound Foolish?" Archives of Internal Medicine, vol 170, no. 4, (February 22, 2010), pp. 340-346.

[40] This report will not use heart failure (HF) or congestive heart failure (CHF) interchangeably. CMS publishes the list of International Classification of Disease Code (ICD) 9 codes that are used to identify heart failure cases (see pp. 27962-27963 of the May 11, 2012, Federal

Register notice.) Other studies may not provide such information. This report will use HF or CHF as indicated by study or context being discussed.

[41] The HF measure was the first readmission measure endorsed by NQF after publication of the proposed FY2009 IPPS rule and before publication of the final FY2009 IPPS rule. As anticipated by CMS, NQF endorsement of the other two readmission measures occurred after publication of final FY2009 IPPS rule and before publication of the CY2009 hospital outpatient prospective payment system (OPPS) rule.

[42] Currently, the public is able to assess the 30-day risk-adjusted readmission rates for a hospital for three conditions as well as whether these rates are the same as, above or below the national average. These measures are calculated using three years of Medicare data; for FY2012, Medicare claims and enrollment data from July 2006 to June 2009 will be used. Hospital COMPARE's outcome of care measures, including condition-specific readmission rates, can be found here: http://data.medicare.gov/dataset/Hospital-Outcome-Of-Care-Measures/f24z-mvb9.

[43] The Reporting Hospital Quality Data for Annual Payment Update (RHQDAPU) initiative was developed as a result of MMA. In 2010, the RHQDAPU program was renamed the Hospital Inpatient Quality Reporting (IQR) Program. See http://www.qualitynet.org/dcs/ContentServer?cid=1138115987129&pagename=QnetPublic%2FPage%2FQnetTier2&c=Page.

[44] See http://www.hospitalcompare.hhs.gov/staticpages/for-consumers/ooc/death-mortality-measures.aspx for readmissions data reported in Hospital COMPARE.

[45] Information on the beneficiary's past medical history and comorbidities are based on diagnoses (ICD-9 codes) on the patient's discharge claim, and are from the hospital inpatient, hospital outpatient, and physician Medicare claims submitted up to 12 months prior to the admission. See http://www.hospitalcompare.hhs.gov/staticpages/forprofessionals/ooc/risk-adjustments-and-covariates.aspx.

[46] The hierarchical generalized linear model accounts for the clustering of patients within hospitals based on the assumption that an individual hospital will provide similar quality of care across patients within its patient population, which can be measured using hospital-specific intercepts. The hospital specific intercepts are given a distribution in order to account for the clustering or non-independence of patients within the same hospital. If there were no differences amoung hospitals, then, after adjusting for patient risk, the hospital intercepts should be identical across all hospitals. The expected number of readmissions in each hospital is estimated using its patient mix and the average hospital-specific intercept (the average of each of the estimated hospital-specific intercepts). The predicted number of readmissions in each hospital is estimated given the same patient mix but the hospital-specific intercept. The excess readmission ratio for a hospital is its predicted number divided by its expected number of readmissions. This is a form of indirect standardization that accounts for variation across hospitals in how sick their patients are when admitted to the hospital and the variation in the number of patients a hospital treats to reveal differences in hospital-specific quality.

[47] Federal Register, August 18, 2011, vol. 76, no 160, pp. 51660-51676. Until FY2015, the hospital readmission program is required to use three readmission measures that were endorsed by NQF as of enactment. At that point,(to the extent practicable), CMS will expand the measures to the four additional conditions identified in MedPAC's June 2007 report. There is no requirement that NQF endorse these additional measures as long as CMS considers such endorsed measures.

[48] This methodology does not try to distinguish preventable admissions, but is an all-cause readmission measure with the following exclusions. All admissions from Medicare disabled beneficiaries under the age of 65 are excluded. The admissions of certain aged Medicare beneficiaries are excluded: those who die in the hospital; those who are subsequently transferred to another acute care facility; those who are discharged against medical advice (AMA); those without at least 30 days post-discharge enrollment in FFS Medicare; and those who are readmitted on the same day to the same hospital with the same condition (patient admission is only counted once). Only the AMI readmission measure will exclude patients who are discharged alive on the same day that they are admitted (because these patients are unlikely to have had a heart attack). Also, the AMI measure will exclude readmissions within 30 days for percutaneous transluminal coronary angioplasty (PTCA) or coronary artery bypass graft (CABG) procedures (because these readmissions likely represent planned readmissions that are part of the same episode of care.) See http://www.hospitalcompare.hhs.gov/staticpages/for-professionals/ooc/data-collection-methods.aspx.

[49] A shorter time interval may provide a greater degree of confidence that a readmission is related to the initial condition. A longer readmission time interval will identify more readmissions. 30-day readmission rates are the most common readmission measure, according to Norbert .I Goldfield,, Elizabeth C. McCullough, John .S. Hughes, Anna.M. Tang, Beth Eastman, Lisa K. Rawlins, and Richard.F Averill, "Identifying Potentially Preventable Readmissions," Healthcare Financing Review, vol 30, no. 1, (Fall 2008), pp. 75-91.

[50] ACA directs the Secretary to use endorsed measures that have exclusions for readmissions that are unrelated to the prior discharge (such as a planned readmission or a transfer to another acute care hospital).

[51] Harold D. Miller, "From Volume to Value: Better Ways to Pay For Health Care," Health Affairs, vol. 28, no. 5 (September/October 2009), pp. 1418-1428.

[52] Sheila Leatherman, Donald Berwick, and Debra Iles, Lawrence S. Lewin, Frank Davidoff, Thomas Nolan, and Maureen Bisognano, "The Business Case For Quality: Case Studies and An Analysis," Health Affairs, vol. 22, no. 2 (March/April 2003), pp. 17-30.

[53] When a patient is discharged or transferred from an IPPS hospital and is readmitted to the same hospital on the same day for symptoms related to, or for the evaluation and management of, the prior stay's medical condition, the two hospital stays are combined. Also, QIOs and other Medicare contractors have the authority to review readmissions for medical necessity and related conditions. CMS Medicare Claims Processing Manual, Chapter 3, Section 40.2.5.

[54] Payments under IPPS depend on the relative resource use associated with a patient classification group, referred to as the Medicare severity (MS) diagnosis related groups (DRG or collectively, MS-DRG), to which the patient is assigned based on an estimate of the relative resources needed to care for a patient with a specific diagnosis and set of care needs. Medicare's IPPS includes adjustments that reflect certain characteristics of the hospital. For instance, a hospital with an approved resident training program could qualify for an indirect medical education (IME) adjustment; hospitals that serve a sufficient number of poor Medicare or Medicaid patients would receive higher Medicare payments because of their disproportionate share hospital (DSH) adjustment. Through FY2012, hospitals located more than 15 miles from another hospital with less than 1,600 total discharges receive a low-volume adjustment. Hospitals in Maryland are not paid using IPPS; rather, they receive Medicare payments based on a state-specific Medicare reimbursement system.

[55] MedPAC, Greater Efficiency, June 2007 pp. 105-106.

[56] 42 CFR 482 contains the COP for hospitals, which are the minimum health and safety standards that hospitals must meet to be Medicare and Medicaid certified. These include, among numerous requirements, requirements related to patients' rights, emergency services, outpatient services, medical record services, and laboratory services. See http://www.cms .hhs.gov/CFCsAndCOP/06_Hospitals.asp#TopOfPage.

[57] Both the discharge plan evaluation and a discharge plan must be developed by, or under the supervision of, a registered professional nurse, social worker, or other appropriately qualified personnel.

[58] Among other requirements related to the discharge plan, the hospital must include, where appropriate, a list of home health agencies or skilled nursing facilities available to the patient, that are participating in the Medicare program and serving the area in which the patient resides or, for skilled nursing facilities, in the geographic area the patient requests.

[59] After analyzing these studies, the authors found that discharge summaries lacked the following information (results were reported as both a median and a range of percentage of occurrences): diagnostic test results, 38% (ranging from 33% to 63%); the treatment or hospital course, 14.5% (ranging from 7% to 22%); discharge medications, 21% (ranging from 2% to 40%); test results pending at discharge, 65% (no range available); and follow-up plans, 14% (ranging from 2%-43%). Sunil Kripalani, Frank LeFevre, and Christopher. O. Phillips, Mark Williams, Preetha Basaviah, David W. Baker, "Deficits in Communication and Information Transfer Between Hospital-based and Primary Care Physicians: Implications for Patient Safety and Continuity of Care," JAMA, vol. 297, no. 8 (February 28, 2007), pp. 831-841.

[60] Ibid.

[61] The study also found that higher discharge summary scores were associated with reduced 30-day readmissions. Alicia Arbaje, Vishnu Surapaneni, Karen Chen, Ivana Vaughn, Kathryn Eubank, and Bruce Leff, "Higher Quality Discharge Summaries of Hospitalized Older Adults are Associated with Reduced Risk of Readmission: Instrument Development and Outcomes," Paper presented at the 2011 Academy Health Annual Research Meeting, Seattle, WA.

[62] Ashish K. Jha, E. John Orav, and Arnold M. Epstein, "Public Reporting of Discharge Planning and Rates of Readmission" NEJM, 2009; 361: 2637-45 examined two different discharge measures to evaluate CHF and PN readmissions to conclude that efforts to publically report data on discharge planning was not likely to yield large reductions in unnecessary admissions.

[63] Performance on the chart-based discharge measure was measured using a scale from 0-100. The authors note that performance criteria were met if the medical record stated that the patient or a caregiver was provided with written instructions or educational material prior to discharge addressing the following: activity level, diet, discharge medications, follow-up appointment, weight monitoring, and what to do if symptoms worsen.

[64] Low correlation between performance evaluated with the two discharge planning measures may be due to the fact that the chart-based measure had information from CHF patients only, while the patient-reported measure had information from all hospitalized medical and surgical patients.

[65] Christopher Phillips, Scott Wright, David Kern, Ramesh Singa, Sasha Sheppard, Haya Rubin, "Comprehensive Discharge Planning With Postdischarge Support for Older Patients With Congestive Heart Failure", JAMA, vol. 291, no. 11 (2004), pp. 1358-67.

[66] Sasha Shepperd, Jacqueline McClaran, Christopher Phillips, Natasha Lannin, Lindy Clemson, Annie McCluskey, Ian Cameron, Sarah Barras, "Discharge Planning from Hospital to

Home", The Cochrane Library, published online January 20, 2010. Available at http://onlinelibrary.wiley.com/doi/10.1002/14651858.CD000313.pub3/abstract.

[67] MedPAC also recommended changes in the enforcement of COP and the correction of provider deficiencies through the development of intermediate sanctions and other interventions. Issues associated with how to define, measure and audit compliance would need to be addressed. MedPAC, "Enhancing Technical Assistance to Providers," June 2011, pp. 107-112.

[68] CMS has been involved with supporting care transitions since 2003, when it joined with the Administration on Aging (AoA) to fund Aging and Disability Resource Center care transitions programs. Local area agencies on aging had been working with Medicare QIOs in some states on the 9th SOW care transitions project.

[69] A QIO support contractor (also called a national coordinating center) leads national efforts to support the local QIOs in achieving the goals of each SOW project. The project support contractor is the contact that sends, receives and disseminates information to the QIOs, collects and reports data, establishes and maintains contacts with national clinical quality improvement experts, and gathers or develops quality improvement tools. The Colorado Foundation for Medical Care (CFMC) was the QIOSC for the 9th SOW care transitions project.

[70] http://www.cfmc.org/integratingcare/toolkit_rca.htm.

[71] Patient activation means that patients have information about their condition, understand warning signs that indicate a clinical deterioration in their health status; patients (or their representatives) know how to advocate for themselves in order to ask appropriate questions. Patient activation also may include a personal health record, an emergency care plan, a pill box or medication manager, and instruction using a "teach-back" method—where the patient explains to a provider or "coach" (in order to ensure that he or she understands) what his or her condition is, what medications are being taken, or other issues.

[72] In the 9th SOW, QIOs developed a number of protocols, standard forms, or best practices to assess patients' health status, routinize discharge procedures and schedule necessary follow-up care.

[73] In the 9th SOW, depending up the locality, QIOs identified care coordination efforts, which could link providers across settings, (data sharing between providers inside and outside the hospital); discharge process improvements, such as notifications given to a patient's primary care physician; and community outreach, which could provide better social supports and assistance tailored to the patient's needs.

[74] In June, 2011, MedPAC recommended that the QIO program be restructured to give providers (and communities) increased choice in who can provide technical quality improvement assistance, to increase competition between these entities, to provide more flexibility in the use of the resources (by direct grants to providers among other changes) and to increase focus on low-performing providers and communities. MedPAC's June 2011, Report to Congress: Medicare and the Health Care Delivery System (subsequently referred to as "MedPAC, "Enhancing Technical Assistance to Providers" June 2011").

[75] As indicated in the 10th SOW, QIOs will provide technical support for the application process which may include: data analyses and trending reports, interventions selection rationale, and cost estimates for interventions and assistance with other application requirements. QIOs will also provide assistance for communities that are not accepted into formal Care Transitions Programs by providing quarterly readmission metrics on various measures (coalition readmission rates; hospital readmission rates, post-acute care setting readmission

rates, disease specific readmission rates, emergency department visit rates, and observation stay rates and mortality rates).

[76] High-risk beneficiaries will be identified using a hierarchical condition category score based on the existence of multiple chronic conditions, previous substandard transitions into post-hospitalization care, or other readmission risk factors which may include cognitive impairment, depression, a history of multiple readmissions, or others factors. The CCTP program is restricted to Medicare FFS beneficiaries including those who are dually eligible (for Medicaid and Medicare).

[77] High readmission hospitals are those with 30-day readmission rates on at least two of the three Hospitals COMPARE measures (HF, AMI, PN) that fall into the top quartile for their state. A listing of the high readmission hospitals can be found at http://www.cms.gov/DemoProjectsEvalRpts/downloads/CCTP_FourthQuartileHospsbyState.pdf.

[78] Eligible CBOs have a governing body that includes sufficient representation of multiple health care stakeholders (including consumers) and provide care transition services across a continuum of care though arrangements with IPPS hospitals. As noted by CMS, CBOs are expected to coordinate across all settings, including hospitals, nursing homes, home health, SNF, and hospice. "Beneficiaries often experience multiple transitions following discharge from the hospital and therefore a CBO must follow that beneficiary across various settings if there is any hope of reducing avoidable admissions." See https://questions.cms.hhs.gov/app/answers/detail/a_id/10602/related/1.

[79] As noted in the CTTP application, participants are expected to reduce Medicare expenditures through the provision of care transition services which would reduce avoidable hospital readmissions. The application must include assumptions regarding overall participation rates, rationale and projections of the readmissions to be avoided, and overall reduction in readmission rates.

[80] http://www.cms.gov/DemoProjectsEvalRpts/MD/itemdetail.asp?itemID=CMS1239313.

[81] https://questions.cms.hhs.gov/app/answers/detail/a_id/10703/kw/Community%20Based%20Care%20Transition%20Program.

[82] The Lewin Group's team includes the Colorado Foundation for Medical Care, the University of Colorado, Seamon Corporation, 371 Productions and ON24.

[83] For summary data on the collaborative network, the prior experience, the target population, the service community, and the implementation strategy of the participants, see http://innovation.cms.gov/initiatives/Partnership-forPatients/CCTP/partners.html.

[84] https://questions.cms.hhs.gov/app/answers/detail/a_id/10600.

[85] https://questions.cms.hhs.gov/app/answers/detail/a_id/10600.

[86] See http://www.caretransitions.org/.

[87] Eric A. Coleman, Carla Parry, and Sandra Chalmers et al., "The Care Transitions Intervention: Results of a Randomized Controlled Trial," Archives of Internal Medicine, vol. 166 (September 25, 2006), pp. 1822-1828.

[88] Carla Parry. Heidi M. Kramer, and Eric A. Coleman, "A Qualitative Exploration of a Patient-Centered Coaching Intervention to Improve Care Transitions in Chronically Ill Older Adults," Home Health Care Services Quarterly, vol. 25, nos. 3 and 4 (2006), pp. 39-53.

[89] See http://www.chcf.org/topics/view.cfm?itemID=128306. Six of the nine grantees that completed the project had specific plans to continue the care transitions work when the project ended in September 2008. The CHCF Care Transitions Projects: Final Progress Report and Meeting Summary, March 2009.

[90] See http://www.transitionalcare.info/.

[91] Mary A. Naylor, Dorothy Brooten,, and Roberta Campbell et al., "Transitional Care of Older Adults Hospitalized with Heart Failure: A Randomized Clinical Trial," Journal of the American Geriatrics Society, vol. 52, no. 5 (May 1, 2004), pp. 675-684.

[92] http://www.hospitalmedicine.org/ResourceRoomRedesign/RR_CareTransitions/PDFs/Workbook_for_Improvement.p df.

[93] The 8P is an eight component screening tool that evaluates 1) problem medications, 2) psychological needs, 3) principal diagnosis, 4) polypharmcy (the potential for adverse reactions when a patient takes multiple drugs); 5) health literacy, 6) patient support, 7) prior hospitalizations, and 8) need for palliative care.

[94] The patient is evaluated in two domains: logistical issues and psychosocial issues using the general assessment of preparedness (GAP) Tool. Depending upon the question, the assessment occurs at admission, prior to discharge, or at discharge.

[95] David Preen, Belinda E. S. Bailey, Alan Wright, Peter Kendall, Martin Phillips, Joseph Hung, Randall Hendriks, Annette Mather, and Elizabeth Williams, "Effects of a Multidisciplinary, Post-discharge Continuance of Care Intervention on Quality of Life, Discharge Satisfaction, and Hospital Length of Stay: A Randomized Controlled Trial." International Journal for Quality in Health Care, vol. 17, no. 1 (2005), pp. 43-51.

[96] See http://www.bu.edu/fammed/projectred/. Louise is a virtual nurse or discharge advocate that runs on a touch screen display as part of a bedside patient education system that is also part of the RED toolkit.

[97] Brian W. Jack, Veerappa K. Chetty, and David Anthony et al., "A Reengineered Hospital Discharge Program to Decrease Rehospitalization," Annals of Internal Medicine, vol. 150, no. 3. (February 3, 2009), pp. 178-187.

[98] A high-risk patient is defined as one who has been admitted two or more times in the past year and failed teach back (could not recall or repeat discharge instructions) or as someone whose family caregiver has a low degree of confidence to carry out self-care at home. Self-care includes weighing self, maintaining diet or adhering to medications, and accessing food, transportation, and medications.

[99] A moderate risk patient is defined as one who has been admitted once in the past year and as someone whose patient or family caregiver has a moderate degree of confidence to carry out self-care at home. Gail A. Nielsen, Annette Bartely, Eric Coleman, Roger Resar, Pat Rutherford, Dan Souw, and Jane Taylor. Transforming Care at the Bedside How-to Guide: Creating an Ideal Transition Home for Patients with Heart Failure. Cambridge, MA: Institute for Healthcare Improvement; 2008. Although the guide addresses the creation of transition homes for patients with heart failure, it is presented as adaptable for patients with other conditions.

[100] Holly L. Lorenz, Pamela K. Greenhouse, Rosemary Miller, Mary K. Wisniewski, and Susan L. Frank, "Transforming Care at the Bedside: An Ambulatory Model for Improving the Patient Experience," The Journal of Nursing Administration, vol. 38, no. 4, (April 2008), pp. 194-199.

[101] Established by the Balanced Budget of 1997, 15 care coordination programs for chronically ill FFS Medicare beneficiaries were started in 2002.The end dates for 11 of the 15 programs were extended from 2006 to 2008; Two of the 11 were further extended through March, 2010, because of their potential for achieving cost neutrality. http://www.cms.gov/DemoProjectsEvalRpts/MD/itemdetail.asp?filterType=none&filterByDID=0&sortByDID=3&sort Order=descending&itemID=CMS1198864&intNumPerPage=2000. Only two programs had a statistically significant effect on the annual number of hospitalizations. No program reduced Medicare program expenditures. The interventions did not systematically

improve process measures of quality of care or patients' health behaviors. Deborah Peikes, Arnold Chen, Jennifer Schore, and Randall Brown, "Effects of Care Coordination on Hospitalization, Quality of Care, and Health Care Expenditures Among Medicare Beneficiaries: 15 Randomized Trials" JAMA, vol. 301, no. 6 (2009), pp. 603-618. (Subsequently referred to as Peikes, et al, "Effects of Care Coordination.")

102 Established by MMA, starting in 2005, the MHS Program tested different care management interventions to improve clinical quality of care and beneficiary/provider satisfaction as well as achieving cost savings for chronically ill Medicare FFS beneficiaries with congestive heart failure or diabetes. Designed in two-phases, after a three-year period, the program or any of its components could be expanded if evaluated as successful according to established measures and conditions. CMS discontinued the program in 2008 after a preliminary evaluation of 18-month interim results. See https://www.cms.gov/CCIP/02_ Highlights.asp and https://www.cms.gov/reports/downloads/ MHS_Second_ Report_to_ Congress_October_2008.pdf.

103 Also, in order to achieve reduced hospitalizations, the programs may want to target patients with intermediate average costs, not those who are relatively healthy or extremely sick. J. Z. Ayanian. "The Elusive Quest for Quality and Cost Savings in the Medicare Program'" JAMA, vol. 301, no. 6 (2009), pp. 668-670. This was also a lesson from MHS program. Michael Barr, Sandra Foote, Randall Krakauer, and Patrick Mattingly, "Lessons for the New CMS Innovation Center from the Medicare Health Support Program" Health Affairs, 29 No. 7 (2010); 1305-1309.

104 Peikes, et al, "Effects of Care Coordination." Also, Rachel Voss, Rebekah Gardner, Rose Baier, Kristen Butterfield, Susan Lehrman, and Stefan Gravenstein, "The Care Transitions Intervention: Translating from Efficacy to Effectiveness," Archives of Internal Medicine, vol. 171, no. 14 (July 2011), pp. 1232-1237. (Subsequently referred to as the Voss study) In this study, Medicare patients who participated in the month-long intervention had 30-day readmission rates of 13% while those who did not participate in the intervention had readmission rates of 20%.

105 In the Voss study, 55% of patients agreed to participate in the intervention and 14% agreed to a home visit. Low participation rates also affected the care coordination programs participating in the MCCD. Peikes, et al, "Effects of Care Coordination."

106 Under the current payment system and typical intervention, the average episode of care costs per patient was determined to be $6,780, while the revenue was $8,196, for a contribution margin of $1,436. With the care transitions program, the episode of care costs was slightly lower, $6,236, while the revenue for the episode of care was also lower, $7,445, for a contribution margin of $1,209. The difference ($1,436-$1,209) in contribution margin was then $227. See Brett Stauffer, Cliff Fullerton, Neil Fleming, Gerald Ogola, Jeph Herrin, Pamala Martin Stafford, and David J. Ballard, "Effectiveness and Cost of a Transitional Care Program for Heart Failure," Archives of Internal Medicine, vol. 171, no. 14 (July 2011), 1238-1243.(Subsequently referred to Stauffer et. al. Effectiveness and Cost of a Transitional Care Program for Heart Failure (2011)).

107 A hospital's financial benefit from a rehospitalization could depend upon whether it had excess bed capacity. One study found that the average length of stay for rehospitalized patients was 0.6 day more than that for comparable patients whose most recent rehospitalization had been at least 6 months previously; although the hospital incurred higher costs when treating rehospitalized patients, Medicare's payments would be approximately the same for both sets of patients. There might be as much financial benefit from rehospitalizations as first time admissions for a hospital with excess capacity, but not

other hospitals. Jencks, Williams, and Coleman, "FFS Medicare Rehospitalizations," NEJM, vol. 360 p. 1427.

[108] In the study by Stauffer noted above, bundled payments would both improve the quality of care for patients and pay for the transitional care programs. However, the bundled payment amount for the index discharge would need to be set higher than current reimbursement rates to appropriately fund these programs. Stauffer et. al. Effectiveness and Cost of a Transitional Care Program for Heart Failure (2011).

[109] Reducing Hospital Readmissions in New York State: A Simulation Analysis of Alternative Payment Incentives, Mathmatica Policy Research, September 2011.

[110] The study examined pay-for-performance (P4P) and episode based payments. The P4P simulation assumed that each hospital would receive a reduced payment if its readmissions exceeded a benchmark. Under episode-based payments the hospitals would receive an enhanced payment for a patient's initial admission, but no payments for subsequent admissions within 30 days.

[111] This appears to be an obstacle for other care transitions programs as well. In fact, one component of Project BOOST (discussed earlier) is designed to help advocates for that program establish at least a revenue-neutral business case for the adoption of that intervention by the hospital See Project BOOST: A Return on Investment Analysis found http://www.hospitalmedicine.org/ResourceRoomRedesign/RR_CareTransitions/PDFs/BOOST_ROI_Paper.final.pdf.

[112] The hospital Value-based Purchasing (VBP) program which will redistribute Medicare payments from low-performing hospitals to high-achieving or improving hospitals based on certain performance measures starting October 1, 2012 is outside the scope of this discussion; readmission measures cannot be included as part of that program. As directed by statute, hospital scores in the VBP program will include an efficiency measure starting in FY2015 that will assess hospital performance based on Medicare spending per beneficiary. This measure will include all spending on hospital patients from three days before admission to 30 days after discharge, including Medicare spending on any rehospitalization. In this respect, the VBP program may provide a general incentive for hospitals to devise and implement strategies to avoid their patients' readmissions.

[113] Section 3025 of ACA also establishes a program, to be administered by the Agency for Healthcare Research and Quality, where patient safety organizations (PSOs) work with high readmission hospitals to improve their readmission rates by March, 2012. See http://www.pso.ahrq.gov/readmin/readmin.htm#general for additional information.

[114] MedPAC identified chronic obstructive pulmonary disease, coronary artery bypass graft surgery, percutaneous transluminal coronary angioplasty and other vascular procedures in addition to PN, HF, and AMI as accounting for almost 30% of potentially preventable readmissions.

[115] The base operating DRG payment amount is determined without regard to the hospital value-based purchasing program and also excludes outlier, IME, DSH, and low-volume hospital payments. Statutory language indicates that hospital-specific payments for sole community hospitals (SCHs) are exempt and payments for Medicare dependent hospitals (MDHs) are exempt for discharges occurring during fiscal years 2012 and 2013. The MDH hospital status will expire on October 1, 2012.

[116] Each rehospitalization during the 30 days following an index admission is considered a readmission, rather than another index admission. However, patients with multiple readmissions are only counted once.

[117] CMS noted that the 30-day time frame "is a clinically meaningful period for hospitals, in collaboration with their medical communities, to reduce readmission risk. This time period for assessing readmission is an accepted standard in research and measurement. We believe that during this 30-day time period, hospital and community partners can take steps to reduce risk by ensuring patients are clinically ready to be discharged, improving communication across providers, reducing risks of infections, and educating patients on symptoms to monitor whom to contact with questions and where and when to seek follow-up care can influence readmission rates." See pp. 51669-70 of the Federal Register, August 18, 2011, vol. 76, no 160.

[118] The Secretary may exempt Maryland hospitals (paid under a Medicare waiver) if the state has a comparable cost-savings program. As discussed in the proposed FY2013 IPPS rule published in the Federal Register on May 11, 2012, Maryland has established a Admission-Readmission Revenue (ARR) Program effective July 1, 2011. CMS will evaluate that voluntary program and determine whether it meets the criteria to exempt Maryland hospitals from HRRP.

[119] "Only a small percentage of 30 day readmissions are probably preventable, and much of what drives hospital readmission rates are patient- and community-level factors outside the hospital's control." Karen Joynt and Ashish Jha, "Perspective: Thirty-Day Readmissions—Truth and Consequences," NEJM, (March 28, 2012).

[120] In March 2012, MedPAC recommended that Medicare payments to SNFs with relative high risk-adjusted rehospitalizations be reduced. Once the risk-adjusted measures have been established, MedPAC recommends that the policy be expanded to cover 30 days after discharge so that SNFs would be encouraged to adopt effective care transitions for patients going home. They contend that these policies will better align hospitals' and SNFs' incentives to reduce rehospitalizations. MedPAC's March 2012, Report to Congress: Medicare Payment Policy, p. 199.

[121] If a hospital is subject to the readmission penalty, Medicare payments for all discharges during the fiscal year will be reduced. The size of the aggregate penalty in any hospital would depend upon the number of Medicare patients served. A hospital with a high Medicare patient load would have a larger financial incentive to dedicate additional resources to preventing readmissions.

[122] In the FY2012 IPPS final rule, CMS stated that it will monitor admissions and readmissions to ensure that there is no systematic shift in patients' primary discharge diagnosis; CMS will consider future monitoring of transfer rates to see if there are unexpected changes in transfer rates. CMS did not mention monitoring trends in observation services provided in hospital outpatient departments.

[123] The Congressional Budget Office has summarized the results from the Medicare Participating Heart Bypass Center Demonstration. The demonstration tested bundled hospital and physician payments for coronary artery bypass graft surgery in select hospitals starting in the early 1990s. See pp. 15-28 of Lessons from Medicare's Demonstration Projects on Value-Based Payment, Congressional Budget Office Working Paper 2012-02, January 2012. at http://www.cbo.gov/ftpdocs/126xx/doc12665/WP2012-02_Nelson_Medicare_VBP_Demonstrations.pdf.

[124] The 'applicable services' are acute care inpatient services, physicians' services delivered in and outside of an acute-care hospital, outpatient hospital services including emergency department services, post-acute services, including home health, skilled nursing, inpatient rehabilitation, long-term care hospital inpatient services, and other services.

125 Quality process, outcome and structure measures will be established to assess: functional status improvement, the reduction of avoidable hospital readmissions, the rates of discharges to the community, the rates of post-hospitalization emergency room admissions, the incidence of health care acquired infections, efficiency measures, measures of patient-centeredness of care, measures of patient perception of care and others.

126 A hospital that is the entity receiving the bundled payment may reduce the number of post-acute providers in its referral network or may increase the use of in-hospital post-acute units to reduce costs or minimize administrative inefficiencies. Neeraj Sood, Peter J. Huckfeldt, Jose J. Escarce, David C. Grabowski, and Joseph P. Newhouse, "Medicare's Bundled Payment Pilot For Acute and Post-acute Care: Analysis and Recommendations on Where to Begin" Health Affairs, vol. 30, no. 9, (September 2011), pp. 1708-1715.

127 Applicants for Model 1 were to submit a non-binding letter of intent by September 22, 2011 and a completed application by October 1, 2011. These dates were changed to October 6, 2011 and November 18, 2011 respectively. Applications for Models 2-4 were originally due by March 15, 2012, but were delayed until June 28, 2012.

128 This will include measuring the spending for included beneficiaries at non-participating providers. According to the RFA, the risk threshold will be set to account for random variation; the methodology will be provided to awardees prior to entering their final agreement.

129 Gainsharing is one of MedPAC's recommended tools to overcome limitations of the current Medicare payment system in order to increase the value for Medicare beneficiaries and taxpayers. See MedPAC, Report to Congress: Improving Incentives in the Medicare Program, Washington, DC, June 2009, p. xii, http://www.medpac.gov/documents/Jun09_EntireReport.pdf.. The March 2011 evaluation of Medicare's gainsharing demonstration programs can be found here: https://www.cms.gov/reports/downloads/Buczko_Gain_Sharing_Final_Report_May_2011.pdf.

130 CMS has established parameters that must be met by the applicant for an acceptable gainsharing arrangement. See pp. 23-24 of the RFA http://innovations.cms.gov/documents/pdf/BundledPayments-Request_for_Application_v5.pdf. (Subsequently referred to as Bundling RFA).

131 This model builds on the ongoing Medicare ACE demonstration where bundled payments are made for all Parts A and B services associated the hospitalization of specified cardiovascular and/or orthopedic procedures in participating sites. See https://www.cms.gov/DemoProjectsEvalRpts/downloads/ACEFactSheet.pdf.

132 CMS will share up to 50% of the Medicare savings with beneficiaries up to a maximum of the annual standard Part B premium, (currently $1,199 in 2012) in the ACE demonstration project. (The exact amount of the ACE shared saving payment to the beneficiary will vary by site and procedure). According to the Request for Applications (RFA), Model 4 will not include sharing savings with patients because past experiences with such policies have proven operationally challenging to administer and confusing for the beneficiaries. Bundling RFA p. 20.

133 Also, experts indicate that efficient and safe hospital discharges are significantly more challenging if appropriate hospital staff are available only during limited daytime hours. Jeffrey L. Greenwald, Charles R. Denham, and Brian W. Jack, "The Hospital Discharge: A Review of a High Risk Care Transition with Highlights of a Reengineered Discharge Process," Journal of Patient Safety, vol. 3, no. 2 (June 2007), pp. 97-106.

134 Up to 41% of general medical patients are discharged from the hospital with pending laboratory tests; as much as 9.4% of the tests results are abnormal and might change patient

care. These pending tests were frequently omitted from the discharge summaries. Stacy Walz, Maureen Smith, and Elizabeth Cox, et al., "Pending Laboratory Tests and the Hospital Discharge Summary in Patients Discharged to Sub-Acute Care," Journal of General Internal Medicine, vol. 26, no. 4 (April 2011), pp. 394-398.

135 Lakshmi Halasyamani, Sunil Kripalani, and Eric Coleman, et al., "Transition of Care for Hospitalized Elderly Patients--Development of a Discharge Checklist for Hospitalists," Journal of Hospital Medicine, vol. 1, no. 6 (November/December 2006), pp. 354-360.

136 Only a quarter of the discharge summaries mentioned any pending tests. Only 13% of the summaries mentioned all pending tests. Follow-up provider information was documented in less than 70% of the summaries. Martin C. Were, Xiaochun Li, and Joe Kesterson, et al., "Adequacy of Hospital Discharge Summaries in Documenting Tests with Pending Rusults and Outpatient Follow-up Providers," Journal of General Internal Medicine, vol. 24, no. 9 (July 2009), pp. 1002-1006.

137 Edward C. Rosenow III, "Patients' Understanding of and Compliance With Medications: The Sixth Vital Sign?" Mayo Clinic Proceedings, vol. 80, no. 8 (August 2005), pp. 983-987.

138 Carolyn M. Clancy, "Patient Engagement in Health Care," Health Services Research, vol. 46, no. 2 (April 2011), pp. 389-393.

139 As noted in the section of the report on CTTP for High Risk Beneficiaries, several of the care transition programs specifically address "red flags" or warning signs that a patient's condition is worsening and steps to take in those cases. For instance, see Eric A. Coleman, Carla Parry, Sandra Chalmers, and Sung-Joon Min, "The Care Transitions Intervention: Results of a Randomized Controlled Trial," Archives of Internal Medicine, 2006;166(17): pp. 1822-8. In the Care Transitions Initiative (CTI), a transition "coach" educates a patient about red flags related to the patient's condition and specific red flags during the hospitalization (symptoms and drug reactions); during a post-discharge home visit (symptoms and adverse effects of medications); as well as during post-discharge telephone calls (instructions regarding when to call a primary care provider).

140 Richard. L. Skolasky, Ariel Frank Green, Daniel Scharfstein, Chad Boult, Lisa Reider, and Stephen T. Wegener, "Psychometric Properties of the Patient Activation Measure Among Multimorbid Older Adults," Health Services Research,vol. 46, no. 2 (April 2011).

141 Gheorghiade et al, "Improving Post Discharge Outcomes' JAMA no. 305, vol. 23, pp. 2456-2457.

142 Most of the studies evaluating the effectiveness of post-discharge calls as an independent intervention have low patient numbers and high risk of bias. Many of the interventions focus on certain diagnoses or localized groups of patients. Also, the primary and secondary outcomes have varied across the studies and have included patient satisfaction, reduction in medication errors, and effect on readmissions or repeat emergency department visits. Spotlight Case: Postdischarge Follow-up Phone Call. WebM&M, March 2012, Agency for Healthcare Research and Quality

143 Published research indicates that most post-discharge phone calls take 10 to 20 minutes. However, depending upon the patient's situation, pharmacists, physicians, and case managers may become involved to identify and address issues and then provide information to the patient's community providers. Ibid.

144 Joseph Ross, M.D., M.H.S.; Gregory Mulvey, Brett Stauffer, Vishnu Patlolla, Susannah Bernhein, Patricia Keenen, Harlan Krumholz, "Statistical Models and Patient Predictors of Readmission for Heart Failure: A Systematic Review," Archives of Internal Medicine, vol. 168, no. 13, (July 14, 2008), pp. 1371-1385. There are key differences between models that seek to predict patient risk of readmission from those that profile and compare hospital

readmission rates. Among other differences, most patient risk models rely on clinical information and laboratory test results while profiling models use more easily accessible administrative data, such as billing information that is submitted on claims. As noted by the authors, most patient risk models accounted for patient characteristics (such as length of stay, discharge disposition, in-hospital events and complications, and patient income education, and race/ ethnicity) that may be inappropriate to include in profiling models . Accounting for such characteristics could inappropriately risk-standardize hospital performance for the differences in quality and efficiency that profiling efforts attempt to measure.

145 Devan Kansagara, Honora Englander, and Amanda Salanitro, et al., "Risk Prediction Models for Hospital Readmission: A Systematic Review," JAMA, vol. 306, no. 15 (October 19, 2011), pp. 1688-1698.

146 Activities of daily living (ADL) are everyday tasks performed by individuals. These include eating, dressing, bathing, getting in and out of bed, and using the bathroom. Instrumental activities of daily living (IADL), which also can be included under the broader ADL category, involve activities related to independent living and include preparing meals, managing money, shopping, doing housework, and using a telephone.

147 Alicia I. Arbage, Jennifer L. Wolff, and Qilu Yu, et al., “Postdischarge Environmental and Socioeconomic Factors and the Likelihood of Early Hospital Readmission Among Community-Dwelling Medicare Beneficiaries,” The Gerontologist, vol. 48 (August 2008), pp. 495-504.

148 Eric A. Coleman, Carla Parry, and Sandra Chalmers, et al., “The Care Transitions Intervention: Results of a Randomized Controlled Trial,” Archives of Internal Medicine, vol. 166 (September 25, 2006), pp. 1822-1828. This study is a randomized control trial and is a follow-up study to an earlier observational study using the same transitional care intervention (using the Care Transitions Initiative) that also showed significant reductions in hospital readmission rates at 30, 90, and 180 days following discharge (see the following footnote).

149 Eric A. Coleman, Jodi D. Smith, Janet C. Frank, Sung-Joon Min, Carla Parry, Andrew M. Kramer, “Preparing Patients and Caregivers to Participate in Care Delivered Across Settings: the Care Transitions Intervention,” Journal of the American Geriatrics Society, vol. 52 (2004), pp. 1817-1825.

150 The term medical error as been defined by the Institute of Medicine as “the failure of a planned action to be completed as intended (an error of execution) or the use of a wrong plan to achieve an aim (an error of planning). An error may be an act of commission or an act of omission”. An adverse event is ”an injury caused by medical management rather than the underlying condition of the patient.” The Agency for Healthcare Research and Quality’s (AHRQ) has developed a framework and set of Patient Safety Indicators, to measure health care quality, including potentially preventable surgical and procedural errors in the inpatient setting. See http://www.qualityindicators.ahrq.gov/Downloads/Software/SAS/V21R2A/psi_guide_rev2.pdf

151 Didem Bernard and William E. Encinosa, “Adverse Patient Safety Events: Costs of Readmissions and Patient Outcomes Following Discharge,” Abstract for AcademyHealth Meeting, San Diego, CA, 2004.

152 p. 51666 of the Federal Register, August 18, 2011, vol. 76, no 160.

153 Stephen F. Jencks, “Rehospitalization: Understanding the Challenge,” Presentation at the National Medicare Readmissions Summit, Washington, DC, June 1, 2009.

[154] Other resources in the after-hospital care plan include a list of tests for which results were not available at the time of discharge, an illustrated description of the patient's diagnosis, and information about what to do if the patient's condition deteriorates. Brian Jack, Veerappa Chetty, David Anthony, Jeffrey Greenwald, Gail Sanchez, Anna Johnson, Shaula Forsythe, Julie O'Donnell, Michael Paasche-Orlow, Christopher Manasseh, Stephen Martin, Larry Culpepper, "A Reengineered Hospital Discharge Program to Decrease Rehospitalization: A Randomized Trial", Annals of Internal Medicine, vol. 150, no. 3 (February 3, 2009), pp. 178-187.

[155] See, for instance, the Care Transitions Initiative, which discusses and practices how to schedule follow-up visits with the patient and provides encouragement to the patient to do so. Rachel Voss, Rebekah Gardner, Rose Baier, Kristen Butterfield, Susan Lehrman, and Stefan Gravenstein, "The Care Transitions Intervention: Translating from Efficacy to Effectiveness," Archives of Internal Medicine, vol. 171, no. 14 (July 2011), pp. 1232-1237.

[156] See the Care Transitions Initiative and the Transitional Care Model, as well as the other care models, listed in Table 1 in the body of this report.

[157] There are a number of programs that could impact the quality of care and likelihood of readmissions for older and disabled adults, including Caregiver Resource Centers, Meals on Wheels, Aging and Disability Resource Centers, and adult day health programs.

[158] Thomedi Ventura, Douglas Brown, Traci Archibald, Alicia Goroski, and Jane Brock, Improving Care Transitions And Reducing Hospital Readmissions: Establishing The Evidence For Community-Based Implementation Strategies Through The Care Transitions Theme, Colorado Foundation for Medical Care (2010) (CFMC) (Ed.).

[159] Marsha Thorson, Jane Brock, Jason Mitchell, and Joanne Lynn. "Grand Junction, Colorado: How a Community Drew on its Values to Shape a Superior Health System," Health Affairs, vol. 29, no. 9 (August 2011), pp. 1678-1686.

[160] See Task C.8 Integrating Care for Populations and Communities, including Improving Care Transitions Leading to the Reduction of Readmissions in the QIOs 10th Statement of Work RFP. QIOs will be evaluated on: 1) recruitment and education of provider groups/communities, 2) coalition building, 3) root cause analysis, 4) plan for intervention selection and implementation, 5) application for participation in a formal Care Transitions Program, 6) ongoing assistance for communities that are not accepted in to a formal Care Transitions Program, and 7) performance measures.

[161] Amy Boutwell, Marian Johnson Patricia Rutherford, et al "An Early Look at A Four-State Initiative to Reduce Avoidable Hospital Readmissions," Health Affairs, vol 30, no. 7 (July 2011) pp. 172-1280. In 4 states (Massachusetts, Michigan, Washington, and Ohio), participating hospitals formed "cross-continuum teams" that involved community agencies, such as SNFs or community-based care providers, as well as representatives of patients and families. Participating hospitals are asked to collect data for all-cause 30-day day hospital readmission rates and to conduct five chart reviews of readmitted patients to identify opportunities to improve transitions .

[162] Jencks, Williams, and Coleman, "FFS Medicare Rehospitalizations." NEJM, vol. 360 pp. 1418-1428.

[163] CMS has solicited public comments with respect to the mechanisms to collect all payer data and the need for common patient identifiers to track patient utilization across providers among other issues in the 2012 IPPS Final Rule. See the August 18, 2001 Federal Register, p. 51673. Also, as the first step of a QIO's root cause analysis, hospitals are required to collect data to analyze the problem and develop solutions. See http://www.cfmc.org/integratingcare/toolkit_rca.html

[164] See p. 109 of MedPAC's Greater Efficiency, June 2007 for a different dissection of potentially preventable medical and surgical admissions and readmissions.

[165] A stent is a tiny tube placed into an artery, blood vessel, or other duct (such as one that carries urine) to hold the structure open. Stents are commonly used to treat coronary heart disease and other conditions that result from blocked or damaged blood vessels.

[166] Chronic obstructive pulmonary disease (COPD) is a progressive disease that makes it difficult to breathe. Chronic bronchitis and emphysema are common examples of COPD.

[167] The pricing component is just one aspect of the program. Geisinger created a new model for CABG surgery with three components: 1) identifying and implementing best practices across the episode of care; 2) developing a risk-based price (which included a 50% discount in the average related postoperative readmission cost); and 3) establishing a patient engagement mechanism (a signed contract where patients agree to actively participate in their care plan). Ronald Paulus, Karen Davis, and Glenn Steele, "Continuous Innovation in Health Care: Implications of the Geisinger Experience," Health Affairs, vol. 27 no 5 (September/October 2008), pp. 1235-1245.

[168] As noted by MedPAC, Geisinger includes all readmissions "not unrelated" in an effort to avoid litigating the difference between 'definitely related' and 'possibly related'. MedPAC, Greater Efficiency, June 2007, p. 108.

[169] Medicare makes payments to most acute care hospitals under the inpatient prospective payment system (IPPS) using a prospectively determined amount for each discharge. A hospital's payment will depend on several factors including the Medicare severity-diagnosis related group (MS-DRG) to which the patient is assigned. See CRS Report R40425, Medicare Primer, coordinated by Patricia A. Davis.

[170] MedPAC, Greater Efficiency, June 2007, p. 108.

[171] Amy E. Boutwell, and Stephen Jencks, "It's Not Six of One, Half-Dozen the Other: A Comparative Analysis of 3 Rehospitalization Measurement Systems for Massachusetts," Presentation given at the 2011 AcademyHealth Annual Research Meeting in Seattle, WA at http://www.academyhealth.org/files/2011/tuesday/boutwell.pdf. (Subsequently referred to as Boutwell and Jencks.)

[172] As noted by MedPAC, its use of 3M's software should be viewed as an examination of a certain approach to defining a preventable readmission and not as an endorsement of a specific product. MedPAC, Greater Efficiency, June 2007, p. 109.

[173] Ibid.

[174] According to this approach, a medical readmission for an acute decompensation of a chronic problem that was not the reason for the initial admission, but was plausibly related to care either during or immediately after the initial admission, is considered to be clinically related to the initial admission - thus potentially preventable. Norbert I. Goldfield, Elizabeth C. McCullough, and John S. Hughes, et al., "Identifying Potentially Preventable Readmissions," Health Care Financing Review, vol. 30, no. 1 (Fall 2008), pp. 75-91. (Subsequently referred to as Goldfield et al, "Identifying Potentially Preventable Readmissions").

[175] MedPAC, Greater Efficiency, June 2007, p 109.

[176] APR-DRGs are determined using the principal diagnosis of each patient or, in the case of surgical patients, the most important surgical procedure that was performed on the patient. See Goldfield et al, "Identifying Potentially Preventable Readmissions."

[177] Goldfield et al, "Identifying Potentially Preventable Readmissions," p. 76.

[178] In a readmission chain, the total time period encompassed can exceed the specified time interval. For example, if the readmission time interval is 15 days, but there are two related

readmissions each 14 days apart, the second readmission would be counted even though it was 28 days from the initial admission. Ibid, p. 78.

[179] See p. 51668 of the Federal Register, August 18, 2011, vol. 76, no 160.

[180] Ibid, p. 51668.

[181] For any given patient none of the subsequent readmissions experienced within the 30 days after the initial index admission would be counted as a new index admission. Ibid, p. 51666.

[182] An index admission is "the admission with a principal diagnosis of a specified condition that meets the inclusion and exclusion criteria for that measure." See http://www.hospitalcompare.hhs.gov/staticpages/help/hospitalglossary.aspx?tool Audience =Hospital&Language=English&TermID=0045 .

[183] For instance, the 30-day AMI readmissions measure does not count as readmissions those admissions after a discharge that include percutaneous transluminal coronary angioplasty (PTCA) or coronary artery bypass graft (CABG) procedures, unless the readmission discharge diagnosis is not consistent with a scheduled readmission: heart failure, AMI, unstable angina, arrhythmia, or cardiac arrest. CMS did not exclude any conditions as planned readmissions for HF or PN, because clinical experts who were consulted did not identify common follow-up causes for a scheduled procedure that would represent continuing treatment care for a HF or PN initial admission. See p. 51667 of the Federal Register, August 18, 2011, vol. 76, no 160.

[184] This is because they would have been unlikely to have had a heart attack. http://www.hospitalcompare.hhs.gov/staticpages/for-professionals/ooc/data-collection-methods.aspx.

[185] There are two other exclusions from all measures: all admissions for beneficiaries under the age of 65 and admissions for beneficiaries who are not in Medicare FFS for at least 30 days following an index discharge.

[186] As stated by CMS, limiting readmissions to particular diagnoses would permit a hospital to avoid countable readmissions by changing coding practices and could also create an incentive to avoid patients with conditions that are part of readmission measures. See p. 51669 of the Federal Register, August 18, 2011, vol. 76, no 160.

[187] As noted by the California Hospital Association, measures that are suitable for public reporting are not appropriate for a payment reduction program. In its view, the bar for accountability should be much higher when hospital payments are at risk. June 20, 2011, IPPS comment letter. p. 13 available at http://www.regulations.gov.

[188] These recommendations were included in various FY2012 IPPS comment letters from different state hospital associations including those from California, Illinois, Massachusetts, and New Jersey, as well as the Association of American Medical Colleges.

[189] See p. 51668 of the Federal Register, August 18, 2011, vol. 76, no 160.

[190] Each rehospitalization during the 30 days following an index admission is considered a readmission, rather than another index admission. Only one readmission for a patient within the 30-day follow-up period is counted. A patient admitted to a hospital with one of the three conditions and then readmitted twice within 30 days of that initial admission would be counted as having one index admission and one readmission.

[191] CMS believes that a three-year period would ensure that the proposed measures would includes a sufficient number of patients (at least 25 cases) to fairly represent the hospital's performance. With the 2006 to 2008 data set, only 2,477 of the 4,476 hospitals had a sufficient number of AMI cases; however, 4,209 hospitals had sufficient HF cases and 4,450 had sufficient number of PN cases. See pp. 51830-51832 of the Federal Register, August 18, 2011, vol. 76, no 160 for the information on the distribution of excess

readmissions by region, hospital bed size, teaching, and urban/rural status. Information from critical access hospitals (CAHs) are included in these tables. According to CMS, the CAH data will be excluded when establishing IPPS readmission program standards.

[192] These are modeled using CMS's Condition Categories based on ICD-9 codes from the patient's discharge claim and from hospital inpatient and outpatient and physician medical claims for the 12 months prior to the patient's admission. If a patient does not have any medical claims for the prior 12 months, then only diagnoses from the index admission are used as part of the risk-adjustment methodology.

[193] The hospital-specific effect is included in the numerator to estimate the adjusted actual admissions. This effect is negative for a hospital with lower than average adjusted rates of admission and positive for a hospital with higher than average adjusted rates of admission (relative to hospitals with similar patients). See pp. 51674-75.of the Federal Register, August 18, 2011, vol. 76, no. 160.

[194] The measures maintenance report does acknowledge that regional differences in resource availability and practice patterns may exert an undue influence on model results. Also, the accuracy of the coding of admission and discharge disposition in the claims data is not known. 2010 Measures Maintenance Technical Report: Acute Myocardial Infarction, Heart Failure, and Pneumonia 30-Day Risk-Standardized Readmission Measures, submitted by Yale New Haven Health Services Corporation: Center for Outcomes Research and Evaluation, March 31, 2010 pp. 9-10, p. 24. (Subsequently referred to as the 2010 Measures Maintenance Report.)

[195] The National Association of Public Hospitals and Health Systems (NAPH), among other hospital industry advocates, encouraged CMS to include additional patient characteristics such as those related to SES that have been observed to be associated with the likelihood of hospital readmissions. According to NAPH, these factors may include race, insurance status, language, health literacy and post-discharge support structure. In their view, race and insurance status were particularly important to include. NAPH FY2012 IPPS comment letter, June 17, 2011, pp. 3-4.

[196] The 2010 Measures Maintenance Report, p. 10.

[197] Federal Register, August 18, 2011, vol. 76, no 160, p. 51670.

[198] The denominator is the number of readmissions (following initial discharges for AMI, HF, PN) that would be anticipated in the particular hospital during the study period, given the patient case mix and the hospital's unique quality of care effect on readmission. The numerator is the number of readmissions (following discharges for AMI, HF, PN) that would be expected if the same patients with the same characteristics had instead been treated at an "average" hospital, given the "average" hospital's quality of care effect on readmission for patients with that condition.

[199] Hierarchical models combine information from all hospitals when estimating the usage rate for a single hospital which adds to the stability of the estimate, particularly for small hospitals. Each hospital's estimate is shrunken toward the overall mean of all hospitals with the amount of the shrinkage greater for hospitals with small sample sizes. This shrinkage adjustment minimizes the reported variance between providers and can make it more difficult for a small volume hospital to be identified as a top hospital. Sean O'Brien, Elizabeth DeLong, and Eric Peterson, "Impact of Case Volume on Hospital Performance Assessment," Archives of Internal Medicine, vol. 168, no. 12 (June 23, 2008), pp. 1277-1284.

[200] Interested parties are more familiar with an observed over expected ratio determined in a logistic regression model. This approach replaces the observed estimate in the numerator

with a predicted estimate that includes the shrinkage adjustment. Also, CMS acknowledges that the hospital-specific effect is not comprehensible to most stakeholders. Arlene Ash, Stephen Fienberg, Thomas Louis, et al, The COPSS-CMS White Paper Committee, Statistical Issues in Assessing Hospital Performance, November 28, 2011. p. 52.

201 Two recent presentations analyzed and compared three different readmissions methods, including the CMS 30-day readmission measure and 3M's potentially preventable readmission measure. See Boutwell and Jencks. See also Sheryl Davies, "Characterizing Hospitals Readmissions in California Inpatient Data" from the same research meeting at http://www.academyhealth.org/files/2011/tuesday/davies.pdf.

202 MedPAC, Greater Efficiency, June 2007, p. 108.

203 See Greater New York Hospital Association, Readmissions advocacy paper available http://www.gnyha.org/3032/Default.aspx.

204 MedPAC, Report to Congress: Medicare Payment Policy, March 2012, p. 69.

205 Robert Berenson, Ronald Paulus, and Noah Kalman, "Perspective: Medicare's Readmissions-Reduction Program – A Positive Alternative," NEJM, vol. 336, no. 15 (April 12 2012), pp. 1364-1365.

In: Hospital Readmissions
Editor: Stephan R. Cox

ISBN: 978-1-62417-283-0

Chapter 2

Readmissions due to Hospital-Acquired Conditions (HACs): Multivariate Modeling and under-coding Analyses*

Richard D. Miller, Jr., Terry Eng, Amy M. G. Kandilov, Jerry Cromwell and Nancy McCall

RTI International#
CMS Contract No. HHSM-500-2005-00029I
August 2012

This project was funded by the Centers for Medicare & Medicaid Services under Contract No. HHSM-500-2005-00029I. The statements contained in this report are solely those of the authors and do not necessarily reflect the views or policies of the Centers for Medicare & Medicaid Services. RTI assumes responsibility for the accuracy and completeness of the information contained in this report.

* This is an edited, reformatted and augmented version of RTI International, dated September 2012.
# RTI International is a trade name of Research Triangle Institute.

Section 1. Introduction and Overview of Research Approach

1.1. Introduction and Findings from Previous Research

This report continues RTI's analysis of the effects of the hospital-acquired conditions-present on admission (HAC-POA) program on utilization, with a specific focus on readmissions. The HAC-POA program was designed to improve the quality of inpatient care to Medicare beneficiaries by providing a negative financial incentive, in which inpatient prospective payment system (IPPS) cases can no longer be assigned to higher-paying MS-DRGs on the basis of reasonably preventable complications or co-morbid (CC) conditions or major complications or co-morbid (MCC) conditions that are acquired during the hospital stay. The reimbursement effects are limited to the initial or index admission only. Thus, even though the hospital may not receive a higher rate of payment for index admissions in which a HAC occurred under the HACPOA program, hospitals could receive additional payments from the Medicare program for care provided during readmissions related to the hospital-acquired condition. A recent study has found that an additional $103 million in payment would be withheld if Medicare expanded the non-payment policy to HAC-related readmissions (see McNair and Luft, 2012).

Previous research has shown to varying degrees that the likelihood of readmission is greater for patients who experience adverse events than for similar patients who have no such adverse events (Ashton et al., 1997; Herwaldt et al., 2006; Encinosa and Hellinger, 2008; Friedman et al., 2009; Friedman and Basu, 2004). Ashton and colleagues (1997) conducted a meta-analysis of the relationship between early readmission rates (31 days) and inpatient processes of care and concluded that substandard care was correlated with higher readmission rates; patients who were readmitted for unplanned reasons were 55% more likely to have had poor quality of care.

Encinosa and Hellinger (2008) studied the occurrence of seven categories of Agency for Healthcare Research and Quality patient safety indicators (PSIs) among 161,004 privately insured patients undergoing surgery. These seven groups of PSIs span the 10 HAC categories included in the HAC-POA program. Excessive 90-day readmission rates, calculated as the difference between the readmission rate estimated if all patients had the PSI and the readmission rate estimated if none of the patients had the PSI, were found for four of the seven PSI groups: infections (7.7%), pulmonary and vascular problems (3.4%), acute respiratory failure (4.3%), and metabolic problems (6.3%).

Infections after surgical procedures are an important reason for early readmissions and have been the focus of a number of recent studies. Herwaldt and colleagues (2006) studied postoperative nosocomial infections associated with general, cardiothoracic, and neurosurgical procedures in a large tertiary care medical center and associated VA hospital. They found that the risk adjusted odds ratio of being readmitted within 30 days of surgery ranged across the three surgical services from 2.15 to 5.62 for patients with a SSI compared with patients with no SSI.

Friedman and colleagues (2009) used an all payer data set of hospitalizations for surgical procedures from seven states and found that the relative risk of readmission was higher for patients experiencing at least one of nine PSIs. The unadjusted rate of 3-month readmission was 25% among patients with a positive PSI compared with 17% among those without a positive PSI. Risk adjustment reduced the 3-month readmission rate differences yet the rates remained statistically higher for patients with each of the nine PSIs.

The most recent literature points to a similar relationship between hospital-acquired conditions and readmissions. Morris et al. (2011) considered unplanned 30-day same-hospital readmissions among 1,808 surgical patients in an urban, tertiary hospital in FY 2009 and found that deep vein thrombosis significantly increased the probability of a readmission, with an odds ratio of 4.7. The reasons for readmission among these patients, however, did not seem to be related to the deep vein thrombosis.

1.2. Summary of Phase II Findings on Readmissions and Potential Estimation Bias

RTI completed a descriptive analysis of the relationship between the Medicare hospital-acquired conditions and readmissions earlier this year (see Kandilov et al., 2012). In that study, we examined the rates and reasons for all-cause readmissions among all discharges in FY 2009 and the first 10 months of FY 2010 in which a HAC was coded by the hospital and the patient was discharged alive. The rates of readmission varied considerably across the different HACs, with the lowest readmission rate for deep vein thrombosis or pulmonary embolism (DVT/PE) following certain orthopedic procedures and the highest readmission rate for blood incompatibility and surgical site infection (SSI) of mediastinitis following a coronary artery bypass graft (CABG) procedure. Readmission rates increased as the readmission window expanded from 7 days to 60 days.

Between FY 2009 and FY 2010, we did not discover any large changes in the readmission rates for any of the HACs, except for among the low-volume surgical site infections, where fluctuations in the readmission rate from year to year likely have more to do with small sample sizes than with actual changes in readmissions for this patient population. Septicemia and pneumonia were among the most common primary diagnoses for readmission across many of the HACs, and for the surgical site infections, post-operative infections were a common reason for readmission. Comparing FY 2009 and FY 2010 data, we did not detect any substantive changes in the reasons for readmission following the development of a HAC during the initial hospitalization.

To address the *incremental* effect of a HAC on readmissions for falls and trauma, vascular catheter-associated infections, and DVT/PE following certain orthopedic procedures, we developed comparison groups for each of the three HACs using a random sample of discharges matched to the HAC cases by key clinical and demographic characteristics. For all three HACs, we found large and statistically significant differences in the readmission rates between the HAC cases and the matched comparison groups. FY 2009 and FY 2010, readmission rates were 3 to 6 percentage points higher for discharges with falls and trauma, 6 to 7 percentage points higher for discharges with a vascular catheter-associated infection, and 2 to 3 percentage points higher for discharges with a DVT/PE following certain orthopedic procedures.

Although we found that readmission rates vary by key patient criteria, such as age, Medicaid status, disability status, and HCC scores, differences in readmission rates between discharges with the HAC and its respective comparison group persisted across most of these stratifications. For patients with a fall or trauma, readmissions remained significantly higher than among the comparison group within all age groups, those with and without Medicaid, all eligibility groups (aged, disabled, ESRD), both genders, within two racial groups (white and other), within all levels of HCC score (low, medium, or high), and within those who were not institutionalized. Significant differences in readmissions also remained when we stratified the vascular catheter-associated infection patients and comparisons by these same categories, and additionally there was a significant difference in readmissions among the black patients. For HACs and comparisons in the DVT/PE group, the only patient characteristics where a significant difference in readmissions did not persist were within patients over 85, those enrolled in Medicaid, those with ESRD, those whose race was other, those who had medium or high HCC scores, and those who were institutionalized.

The significant differences in readmission rates also persisted when we stratify by important hospital characteristics such as Census division, urban location, teaching status, and bed size. For falls and trauma, the rate of readmissions was significantly higher for the HAC cases than for the control cases across all of these stratifications of hospital characteristics. For vascular catheter-associated infections, readmission rates for HAC cases were also significantly higher within all Census divisions, urban and rural hospitals, teaching and non-teaching hospitals, and for hospitals with 100-299 beds and hospitals with 300 or more beds.

While the rates of readmission for the beneficiaries who acquired one of the three conditions during their hospitalization were much higher than for comparison beneficiaries, we found many of the same reasons for readmission for these two groups across our two years of data. The primary exception was the "infection of a central venous catheter," which was one of the top five reasons for readmission among those with a hospital-acquired vascular catheter- associated infection, while it was not among the top reasons for readmission among the comparison group beneficiaries.

Finally, we created a separate study sample to conduct further investigations of mediastinitis following coronary artery bypass graft (CABG) surgery. The number of mediastinitis cases that were HACs is very small so we undertook this study to examine the possible degree of under-reporting of mediastinitis during the hospital period or clinical presentation of mediastinitis after discharge. The primary motivation for this study was to examine the degree to which readmission estimation bias may exist due to identification errors in the dependent variable because of either under-reporting of the HAC by the hospital or a delay in clinical presentation until after discharge.

The mediastinitis study sample included all discharges with a CABG procedure in either FY 2009 or FY 2010. We linked the MedPAR records for these discharges with all physician claims billed during the admission and all physician and hospital outpatient department claims for a 60-day follow-up period and explored the reporting of mediastinitis by physicians during the hospitalization and follow-up periods.

Of the 195 cases of mediastinitis identified during the index hospitalization using a hospital or physician diagnosis, 65% were coded only on the physician claims, and 21% were coded only on the hospital claims. The rate of agreement between hospital and physician coding of mediastinitis was poor, with only 14% of all mediastinitis cases identified in the hospital coded on both hospital and physician claims. Most physician-reported diagnoses of mediastinitis occurred between day 9 and day 23 following the CABG surgery. The first physician diagnosis of mediastinitis was most likely to be made by an infectious disease specialist.

Overall, we found low rates of reporting of mediastinitis by physicians after discharge from the hospital. However, the rate of observed interactions between the patient and their primary surgeon post-discharge was extremely low; only 14 out of 149,395 Medicare beneficiaries had a follow-up appointment within 30 days. This low number is likely a reflection of the global billing payment policy. Thus, it would appear that the use of Medicare claims with the global billing convention may not be an adequate source of information to conduct post-discharge analyses for beneficiaries having major surgical procedures subject to the global surgical payment policy.

1.3. Overview of Phase III Research Questions and Analytic Approach

The readmission multivariate analyses presented in this report represent an extension of the descriptive analysis of readmissions that we completed in Phase II of the study. The Phase III research questions that we address in this study are:

- Does the likelihood of readmission differ between cases that report HACs and similar cases that do not report HACs?
- Does the likelihood of use of post-acute care (PAC) services differ between cases that report HACs and similar cases that do not report HACs?

We use a two stage estimation strategy for readmissions. The first stage is the estimation of a single period, mixed-effects level model where logistic regression is used to estimate the likelihood of having a readmission within 30 days of discharge. A dichotomous variable is included for the presence or absence of a HAC (1 = HAC; 0 = no HAC). We report the odds ratio (OR) on the presence of a HAC from the logistic regressions along with an indication of the level of statistical significance of the effect. Odds ratios greater than 1.0 indicate an increased likelihood of a readmission; odds ratios less than 1.0 indicate a decreased likelihood of a readmission.

In the second stage, we replicate the method of Encinosa and Hellinger (2008) and report the excess likelihood of readmission associated with HAC status and its associated standard error using the multivariate logistic regression models developed in the first stage. In general, the strategy is to use the results of the logistic regression models to estimate the likelihood of readmission assuming that all hospitalizations had an adverse event (HAC) and then estimate the likelihood of readmission assuming that all hospitalizations had no adverse event (no HAC). The difference between the two sets of predictions is the "excess" likelihood of readmission that can be attributed to the HAC after controlling for hospital- and patient-level characteristics, including co-morbidities.

To better understand the role of post-acute care services in observed readmission rates, we also estimate the single-period, multilevel model on the likelihood of any post-acute care services following the general estimation strategy for readmissions. We do not generate estimates of the "excess" likelihood for PAC admissions, but do report the odds ratios from the logistic regressions. We also provide descriptive statistics regarding the relationship between two discharge destinations (PAC and home) and the likelihood of readmission. These analyses consider this relationship for patients both with and without HACs present.

We also conduct a special study which is an extension of last year's work to examine the degree to which readmission estimation bias may exist due to identification errors in the dependent variable because of either under-reporting of the HAC by the hospital or a delay in clinical presentation until after discharge. The Phase III research questions that we address in this special study are:

- What proportion of HAC cases are identified during the index hospitalization period from physician claims and what is the degree of concordance with the MedPAR claim diagnosis for these HACs?
- What is the typical timing to a physician diagnosis of a HAC-related condition during a hospitalization? And what proportions of patients with a HAC and without a HACrelated condition are diagnosed on a subsequent inpatient claim within 7, 15, or 30 days following hospital discharge?
- What evidence do we find of treatment for an infection among the outpatient department drug claims for patients at-risk of developing a HAC-related infection within 30 days following discharge?

To conduct further investigation of potential under-coding or post-discharge presentation of the more frequent HACs, we conducted a series of descriptive analyses. To analyze the potential degree of under-coding during the hospitalization, we compare the degree of concordance in coding a HAC between hospital claims and linked physician claims for the hospitalization period. We examined the timing between procedures that put patients at risk of developing a HAC and physician diagnosis of the HAC-related conditions in the hospital, and we also analyzed post-discharge presentation of the HAC-related conditions by linking hospital, SNF, IRF, and LTCH claims in the 30-days following the index hospitalization to the index hospital claim and reporting the 7-, 15-, and 30-day readmission rates for patients at risk of developing the HAC during the hospitalization and for those that have a HAC reported. We do not include physician or hospital outpatient department (OPD) claims in this analysis as the rate of follow-up for patients with a major surgical procedure that puts them at risk of developing a HAC is extremely low during the post-discharge period due to the Medicare global surgical payment policy that does not allow physicians to routinely bill for services within 90 days of the procedure that are related to follow-up care for the procedure. For the infection-related HACs, we also linked outpatient department drug claims within a 30-day period of discharge and report the percentage of beneficiaries who received antibiotics that would be appropriate for treatment of a HAC-related infection.

1.4. Organization of Report

Section 2 of this report describes the study sample, data, and methods to answer the first two research questions related to likelihood of readmission and likelihood of PAC transfer for patients with a HAC and those at risk for development of a HAC but for whom no HAC is recorded during the hospital stay. Section 3 provides results of the multivariate modeling of readmission. Section 4 provides descriptive and multivariate analyses of likelihood of using PAC services. Section 5 describes the study sample, data, methods, and presents the results of the special study of potential under-coding and time to clinical presentation for selected HACs. Section 6 presents a summary of the findings.

Section 2. Technical Approach

2.1. Study Sample and Data

For the analysis of readmissions among patients with hospital-acquired conditions (HACs), we created our study sample by linking Medicare claims data to "index" HAC inpatient prospective payment system (IPPS) hospital claims. These "index" claims were defined as claims with the HAC-associated diagnoses coded as not present on admission (POA indicator = "N" or "U"). The index HAC claims were taken from MedPAR files for FY 2009 and the first ten months of FY 2010, to allow for a 60-day look-forward period. From these index HAC claims, we used a cross-referenced beneficiary identifier (HIC number) to look back 180 days prior to the index admission date in order to identify any Medicare claims (inpatient, outpatient, home health, and physician claims) for that patient within that period. The claims data for the look-backs came from FY 2008, FY 2009, and FY 2010, as needed. These look-back claims were used to calculate concurrent Hierarchical Condition Category (HCC) indicators for these patients, which were then used to generate indicators of pre-existing medical conditions as described in ***Section 2.7***. We then used the HIC number to look forward 30 days from the index discharge date for additional hospital admissions. If a patient was discharged from their index HAC hospitalization and admitted to another IPPS hospital within a day (with a discharge designation of an acute care transfer), then the 60-day follow up period began with the discharge date from that second transfer hospitalization.

The study sample was limited to beneficiaries who were residents of the U.S., who were enrolled in Medicare Parts A & B, who did not have Medicare as a secondary payer, and who were *not* enrolled in managed care during their HAC index claim, during the 180 days prior to the index admission, and during the 30-day period following the index discharge. The sample was also limited to patients who were discharged alive from their index hospitalization. These exclusions allowed us to focus on Medicare patients with HACs who could possibly have a readmission and whose readmission claims we would likely find using MedPAR claims data. For example, if a Medicare beneficiary with an index HAC admission switched to Medicare managed care during the 60-day follow-up period, any hospital readmissions they might have had would not be present in the MedPAR claims data. Including these beneficiaries in the sample could lead to an under-estimation of the readmission rates.

2.2. Defining Readmissions

For the statistics presented in this report, we use a measure of hospital all-cause readmissions and include all admissions to acute care hospitals that occur within 30 days of the index claim discharge date, regardless of the clinical reason for the admission. In addition to IPPS hospitals, an admission to a critical access hospital (CAH) or to another non-IPPS hospital that is paid under Medicare Part A (such as a Cancer hospital or a Children's hospital) following an index IPPS hospital discharge is considered a readmission. This measure of readmissions does not include admissions to an inpatient rehabilitation facility (IRF) or to a long-term care hospital (LTCH), which are included among our measure of post-acute care. Discharges from the index hospitalization to another acute care IPPS hospital, where the index discharge date is within one day of the next admission date and the discharge destination is a transfer, are treated as transfer cases and so are not included as readmissions. The 30-day look-forward period begins with the discharge date of the transfer hospitalization, if there is one.

2.3. Defining Discharges to PAC Settings

For the analyses of post-acute care utilization, we created a measure based on the discharge destination variable in the MedPAR data. The following settings were included in our PAC definition: skilled nursing facilities, organized home health service organizations, intermediate care facilities, inpatient rehabilitation facilities, and long-term care hospitals.

2.4. Selection of the Three Study HACs

Based on our initial descriptive statistics produced for the Strategic Memo: Strategy to Estimate Readmissions Due to Hospital-Acquired Conditions (HACs), we selected three HACs from the current set of HACs for further analysis in this report. The primary criterion for our selection was that the chosen HACs have a sufficient volume to estimate statistically reliable descriptive statistics, allowing us to examine variation in readmission rates across beneficiary characteristics. Using this criterion, we selected the following three HACs for the Phase II report:

- ***Falls and trauma***, with 7,954 HAC-associated live discharges in FY 2009 and the first 10 months of FY 2010.
- ***Deep vein thrombosis or pulmonary embolism (DVT/PE)*** following certain orthopedic procedures, with 4,195 HAC-associated live discharges in FY 2009 and the first 10 months of FY 2010.
- ***Vascular catheter-associated infection*** with 5,167 HAC-associated live discharges in FY 2009 and the first 10 months of FY 2010.

We continue to analyze these three HACs in this Phase III report.

2.5. Comparison Group Matching Criteria

To develop a valid comparison group we selected discharges based on a small set of clinical or demographic characteristics held in common with the specific HAC cases, and then used a larger set of covariates in the outcome regressions. Matching is a common technique found among empirical studies on this topic. For the descriptive analysis in this report, we took a multivariable matching approach. Multivariable matching uses a limited number of specific characteristics and identifies controls that match on *all* of the variables.

To construct appropriate comparison groups for the three selected study HACs, we matched each index claim identified with a HAC to 10 IPPS claims without a HAC but with the same MS-DRG and demographic characteristics (sex, race, and age) as the HAC claim. In the cases where a 10:1 match was not obtainable, we reweighted the matches that were made to simulate a 10:1 match. Any claims with the HAC-associated diagnosis codes identified as present on admission (POA indicator equal to "Y" or "W") were excluded from the comparison group, since conditions coded as present on admission could potentially be true HACs that were miscoded. Including true HACs in the comparison group could introduce bias in our results. Thus, the comparison group for each of the three HACs contained no index claims with the specified HAC-associated diagnoses.

No additional restrictions were placed on the comparison group for the falls and trauma HACs. For the DVT/PE following certain orthopedic procedures, the set of claims from which the comparison group was drawn was further limited to those claims containing the orthopedic procedure associated with this HAC. To better target the population who would be at risk for a vascular catheter-associated infection, we limited this comparison group to index claims that had one of two vascular catheter procedure codes (38.93 or 38.95). Note that among patients with the vascular catheter-associated infection HAC, 38% did not have a vascular catheter procedure code on their claims. The vascular catheter codes may have been coded after the fifth surgical procedure code, and thus not picked up by the MedPAR data, or may have been left off of the claim completely. Readmission rates were similar between the HAC claims that included the vascular catheter procedure codes and those that did not include the codes.

From these index comparison claims, we linked additional claims data both before and after the index comparison claim, as described in *Section 2.1*, in order to calculate readmission rates and co-morbid conditions. The same sample exclusions – residents of the U.S., enrolled in Medicare Parts A & B, Medicare not the secondary payer, and not enrolled in managed care – were applied to the identified comparison groups to ensure analogous samples.

2.6. Multivariate Analyses

To estimate the impacts of each of the three study HACs on the likelihood of readmission within 30 days, we estimated mixed effects (or multi-level) logistic models. The mixed effects models are necessary due to the multi-level nature of the data being analyzed. The idea is to control for both patient- or discharge-level covariates such as co-morbid conditions and age as well as hospital-level covariates such as size (number of beds). Also, the discharges are clustered within hospitals, so it is necessary to model this clustering.

The mixed effects logistic model is derived through using the logistic function to model the probability of readmission based on the value of a latent variable, where Y_{ij} indexes discharges within hospitals and j indexes hospitals.

$$Pr_{ij}(\text{Readmission}) = 1 / [1+\exp(-Y_{ij})]$$

The variable Y_i can be thought of as a function of HAC status as well as other patient- or discharge-level characteristics (X) and an individual-level error term (r) as follows:

$$Y_{ij} = \beta_0 + \beta_1 HAC_{ij} + \beta_2 X_{ij} + r_{ij}$$

The mixed effects model is implemented by allowing the βs to vary across hospitals, which constitute a second level of data. We considered three different specifications for modeling the likelihood of readmission for each of the three HACs and the likelihood of discharge to a PAC setting. The first was a random intercept model. The second was a random intercept model where we allowed the intercept to be a function of hospital-level covariates. The third was a model, which built upon the second model by estimating a random effect for the HAC indicator variable.

Model I

$$\text{Level 1: } Y_{ij} = \beta_{0j} + \beta_1 HAC_{ij} + \beta_2 X_{ij} + r_{ij}$$

$$\text{Level 2: } \beta_{0j} = \gamma_{00} + u_{0j}$$

In this case the intercept term is equal to an average intercept across all hospitals and a hospital-specific random error term (u_{0j}). The model may be re-written as one equation as follows:

$$Y_{ij} = \gamma_{00} + \beta_1 HAC_{ij} + \beta_2 X_{ij} + r_{ij} + u_{0j}$$

This model is composed of fixed effects (the γ_s and β_s) and random effects (the random error terms).

Model II

$$\text{Level 1: } Y_{ij} = \beta_{0j} + \beta_1 HAC_{ij} + \beta_2 X_{ij} + r_{ij}$$

$$\text{Level 2: } \beta_{0j} = \gamma_{00} + \gamma_{01} W_j + u_{0j}$$

In this case the intercept term is a function of hospital-level covariates (W_j) and a hospital-specific random error term (u_{0j}). The model may be re-written as one equation as follows:

$$Y_{ij} = \gamma_{00} + \gamma_{01}W_j + \beta_1 HAC_{ij} + \beta_2 X_{ij} + r_{ij} + u_{0j}$$

This model is composed of fixed effects (the γ_s and β_s) and random effects (the random error terms).

Model III

Level 1: $Y_{ij} = \beta_{0j} + \beta_{1j} HAC_{ij} + \beta_2 X_{ij} + r_{ij}$

Level 2: $\beta_{0j} = \gamma_{00} + \gamma_{01}W_j + u_{0j}$

$\beta_{1j} = \gamma_{10} + u_{1j}$

In this case the intercept term is a function of hospital-level covariates (W_j) and a hospital-specific random error term (u_{0j}). The coefficient on the HAC indicator is equal to the average value of the coefficient across all hospitals (γ_{10}) and a hospital-specific random error term (u_{1j}). The model may be re-written as one equation as follows:

$$Y_{ij} = \gamma_{00} + \gamma_{01}W_j + \gamma_{10} HAC_{ij} + \beta_2 X_{ij} + r_{ij} + u_{0j} + u_{1j}$$

This model is composed of fixed effects (the γ_s and β_s) and random effects (the random error terms).

In each of the specifications, we control for the following discharge- or patient-level characteristics (the Xs): age, Medicaid enrollment, original eligibility status, gender, race, institutional status, and several co-morbid conditions (we discuss the measures for co-morbid conditions in ***Section 2.7***). In the Models II and III, we control for the following hospital-level characteristics (the Ws): whether the hospital is located in an urban area, number of beds, and whether the hospital is an academic medical center (teaching hospital).

2.7. Co-morbid Condition Measures

To control for co-morbid conditions in our models, we included a series of indicator variables suggested in a report to CMS by the Yale New Haven Health Services Corporation/Center for Outcomes Research and Evaluation (referred to as Yale for the remainder of this report). Based on several factors, the Yale team grouped CMS condition categories (CMS-CCs) into a series of 31 co-morbid risk variables.[1]

The grouping of the CMS-CCs into the risk variables is presented in ***Table 2-1***.

Table 2-1. The Yale co-morbid condition measures

Co-morbid condition measure	CMS Co-morbid conditions included
Severe infection	1 HIV/AIDS 3 Central nervous system infection 4 Tuberculosis 5 Opportunistic infections
Other infectious disease	6 Other infectious disease 111 Aspiration and specified bacterial pneumonias 112 Pneumococcal pneumonia, emphysema, lung abscess 113 Viral and unspecified pneumonia, pleurisy
Metastatic cancer/acute leukemia	7 Metastatic cancer/acute leukemia
Severe cancer	8 Lung, upper digestive tract, and other severe cancers 9 Other major cancers
Other major cancers	10 Breast, prostate, colorectal and other cancers and tumors 11 Other respiratory and heart neoplasms 12 Other digestive and urinary neoplasms
Diabetes mellitus	15 Diabetes with renal manifestation 16 Diabetes with neurologic or peripheral circulatory manifestation 17 Diabetes with acute complications x 18 Diabetes with ophthalmologic manifestation 19 Diabetes with no or unspecified complications 20 Type I diabetes mellitus 119 Proliferative diabetic retinopathy and vitreous hemorrhage 120 Diabetic and other vascular retinopathies
Protein-calorie malnutrition	21 Protein-calorie malnutrition
End-stage liver disease	25 End-Stage Liver Disease 26 Cirrhosis of Liver
Other hematological disorders	44 Other hematological disorders
Drug and alcohol disorders	51 Drug/alcohol psychosis 52 Drug/alcohol dependence
Psychiatric comorbidity	54 Schizophrenia 55 Major depressive, bipolar, and paranoid disorders 56 Reactive and unspecified psychosis 58 Depression 60 Other psychiatric disorders
Hemiplegia, paraplegia, paralysis and functional disability	67 Quadriplegia, other extensive paralysis 68 Paraplegia 69 Spinal Cord Disorders/Injuries 100 Hemiplegia/hemiparesis

Table 2-1. (Continued)

Co-morbid condition measure	CMS Co-morbid conditions included
	101 Diplegia (upper), monoplegia, and other paralytic syndromes 102 Speech, language, cognitive, perceptual 177 Amputation status, lower limb/amputation 178 Amputation status, upper limb
Seizure disorders and convulsions	74 Seizure disorders and convulsions
Congestive heart failure	80 Congestive heart failure
Coronary atherosclerosis or angina, cerebrovascular disease	81 Acute myocardial infarction 82 Unstable angina and other acute ischemic heart disease 83 Angina pectoris/old myocardial infarction 84 Coronary atherosclerosis/other chronic ischemic heart disease 89 Hypertensive heart and renal disease or encephalopathy 98 Cerebral atherosclerosis and aneurysm 99 Cerebrovascular disease, unspecified 103 Cerebrovascular disease late effects, unspecified 104 Vascular disease with complications 105 Vascular disease 106 Other circulatory disease
Specified arrhythmias	92 Specified heart arrhythmias 93 Other heart rhythm and conduction disorders
COPD	108 Chronic Obstructive Pulmonary Disease
Dialysis status	130 Dialysis status
Ulcers	148 Decubitus ulcer 149 Decubitus ulcer or chronic skin ulcer
Septicemia/shock	2 Septicemia/shock
Cardio-respiratory failure and shock	79 Cardio-respiratory failure and cardio-respiratory shock
Acute renal failure	131 Acute renal failure
Pancreatic disease	32 Pancreatic disease
Rheumatoid arthritis and inflammatory connective tissue disease	38 Rheumatoid arthritis and inflammatory connective tissue disease
Respirator dependence	77 Respirator dependence/tracheostomy status
Transplants	128 Kidney transplant status 174 Major organ transplant status
Hip fracture/dislocation	158 Hip fracture/dislocation

Source: Horwitz et al. (2011).

Section 3. Multivariate Results for Likelihood of Readmission Within 30 Days of Discharge

3.1. Choosing among Potential Model Specifications

We estimated three separate specifications or models to estimate the impact of HAC status on the likelihood of readmission, while controlling for patient and hospital characteristics. In this section, we provide a rationale for the choice of final specification that we made for each of the three HACs considered in this study. The results for the three specifications for each HAC can be found in ***Appendix Tables 1*** through ***3***.

Falls and Trauma

The result regarding the effect of having a HAC on the likelihood of readmission within 30 days is quite consistent across all three specifications. This is also true for the effect of the control variables. Including the hospital-level covariates has very little impact on the coefficients for the patient- or discharge-level covariates, although at least some of the hospital-level covariates are significant.

In all three models, the random effect on the intercept is significant. At the same time, only roughly 7% of the total variance is determined to be due to differences in readmission rates across hospitals. In Model III, the random effect on the HAC indicator is not significant and neither is the covariance between the intercept and the HAC indicator. Allowing for the random effect on the HAC indicator has no significant impact on the results. Based on these results, we report the results from Model II for falls and trauma.

Vascular Catheter-Associated Infection

Again, the result regarding the effect of having a HAC on the likelihood of readmission within 30 days is quite consistent across all three specifications. This is also true for the effect on the control variables. Including the hospital-level covariates has very little impact on the coefficients for the patient- or discharge-level covariates, although at least some of the hospital-level covariates are significant.

In all three models, the random effect on the intercept is significant. At the same time, only roughly 5% of the total variance is determined to be due to differences in readmission rates across hospitals. In Model III, the random effect on the HAC indicator is not significant and neither is the covariance between the intercept and the HAC indicator. Allowing for the random effect on the HAC indicator has no significant impact on the results. Based on these results, we report the results from Model II for vascular catheter-associated infection.

DVT/PE Following Certain Orthopedic Procedures

In this case, the result on the effect of having a HAC is quite different when allowing for a random effect on the HAC indicator in Model III. In addition, the random effect on the HAC indicator is quite significant. Based on the significance of the random effect on the HAC indicator, we report the results from Model III for DVT/PE.

3.2. Logistic Model Results

The results of the chosen mixed effects logistic model for each HAC are presented in ***Table 3-1***. The main finding is that the presence of each HAC has a significant positive impact on the likelihood of readmission within 30 days. For the falls and trauma HAC and the DVT/PE HAC, the presence of the HAC is associated with a 21 to 23% increase in the odds of being readmitted within 30 days, respectively. The presence of the vascular catheter-associated infection HAC has an even greater impact on the likelihood of readmission. It is associated with a 33% increase in the odds of being readmitted within 30 days. As far as the hospital-level covariates are concerned, larger hospitals tend to have higher readmission rates. For instance, in the falls and trauma sample, the odds ratio for the largest hospitals (those with 300 or more beds) is equal to 1.139, which indicates that the odds of a readmission are 14% higher for patients from these larger hospitals than for patients from hospital with fewer than 100 beds. The effect of hospital size is largest for patients in the DVT/PE sample, or almost 40% higher. There is no association between bed size and likelihood of readmission for patients at risk to develop a DVT or PE. Discharges from academic medical centers are also associated with a higher likelihood of readmission for patients at risk of a fall or trauma, 18%, and vascular catheter-associated infection, 22%. The results of the influence of level of urbanicity are mixed. Urbanicity has no correlation with the likelihood of readmission in the falls and trauma sample. At the same time, discharges from urban hospitals are associated with a higher likelihood of readmission in the vascular catheter-associated infection sample, 10%, and with a lower likelihood of readmission in the DVT/PE sample, 12%.

The results on patient age are also mixed. In the falls and trauma and DVT/PE samples, there is a positive relationship between age and the likelihood of readmission after controlling for other factors, including co-morbidities. In the vascular catheter-associated infection sample, there is to be a negative relationship. The effect of Medicaid enrollment is more consistent across the three samples. In each case, Medicaid enrollment is associated with a greater likelihood of readmission. In the DVT/PE sample, the odds of readmission is 35% higher for Medicaid enrollees than for non-enrollees, while for the falls and trauma and vascular catheter-associated infection samples, the odds of readmission among Medicaid enrollees are 20 and 15% higher, respectively. Among the discharges in the falls and trauma and DVT/PE samples, original Medicare eligibility status and gender are important determinants of the likelihood of readmission. Patients who initially became eligible for Medicare due either to disability or ESRD status have a greater likelihood of readmission than patients who initially became eligible due to age. Women generally have a lower likelihood of readmission than men. In the falls and trauma sample, the odds of readmission were 9% lower for women than for men and in the DVT/PE sample, the odds of readmission were more than 20% lower. Generally, race and institutional status have no effect on the likelihood of readmission. Co-morbidities are very important determinants of the likelihood of readmission. In each sample, at least one-half of the Yale co-morbidity measures have significant odds ratios. In all cases where the odds ratios are significant, the odds ratio is greater than one, indicating that the co-morbidities are associated with a greater likelihood of readmission.

Table 3-1. Multivariate regression estimates of the likelihood of a 30-day readmission for selected hospital-acquired conditions (HAC)

Falls and trauma		Vascular catheter-associated infection	DVT/PE following certain orthopedic procedures
Variable	(n=78,827)	(n=44,981)	(n=41,432)
HAC Indicator	**1.214****	**1.330****	**1.229****
Hospital-Level Covariates			
Urban	0.998	1.096*	0.875*
Number of beds (reference is "fewer than 100"			
100-299	1.112**	1.028	1.376**
300 or more	1.139**	1.097	1.393**

Table 3-1. (Continued)

Falls and trauma		Vascular catheter-associated infection	DVT/PE following certain orthopedic procedures
Variable	(n=78,827)	(n=44,981)	(n=41,432)
Academic medical center	1.175**	1.218**	1.109
Discharge-Level Covariates			
Age (reference is "less than 65")			
65-74	0.989	0.950	1.078
75-84	1.106*	0.893*	1.682**
85 and older	1.225**	0.779**	2.371**
Enrolled in Medicaid	1.197**	1.145**	1.346**
Original eligibility (reference is "aged")			
Disabled	1.092**	1.020	1.348**
ESRD	1.558**	1.080	2.091**
Gender: Female	0.910**	1.033	0.771**
Race (reference is "white")			
Black	0.960	0.960	0.984
Asian	0.891	1.018	0.876
Other	0.915	0.952	0.915
Institutionalized	0.778	0.823	0.400
Yale Comorbidity Measures			
Severe infection	1.089	1.222*	0.510
Other infectious disease	1.142*	1.059	1.122
Metastatic cancer/acute leukemia	1.286**	1.260**	1.662*
Severe cancer	1.235**	0.993	1.226
Other major cancers	1.039	0.967	0.876
Diabetes mellitus	1.182**	1.134**	1.132*
Protein-calorie malnutrition	1.152**	0.987	1.503**
End-stage liver disease	1.368**	0.953	2.346**
Other hematological disorders	1.404**	1.160**	1.099
Drug and alcohol disorders	1.410**	1.116	1.789**
Psychiatric comorbidity	1.121*	1.185**	1.148
Hemiplegia, paraplegia, paralysis and functional disability	1.175**	1.027	1.124
Seizure disorders and convulsions	1.100	1.121*	1.674**
Congestive heart failure	1.331**	1.113**	1.353**
Coronary atherosclerosis or angina, cerebrovascular Disease	1.147**	1.076*	1.222**
Specified arrhythmias	1.120**	1.053	1.101
COPD	1.328**	1.072*	1.381**
Dialysis status	1.242**	1.181**	0.997
Ulcers	1.138**	0.973	1.389*
Septicemia/shock	1.127**	1.147**	1.282
Cardio-respiratory failure and shock	1.057	1.068	1.017
Acute renal failure	1.342**	1.230**	1.657**

Falls and trauma		Vascular catheter-associated infection	DVT/PE following certain orthopedic procedures
Variable	(n=78,827)	(n=44,981)	(n=41,432)
Pancreatic disease	1.254**	1.217**	1.427
Rheumatoid arthritis and inflammatory connective tissue disease	1.178**	1.127**	1.314**
Respirator dependence	1.497**	1.074	5.516**
Transplants	1.560**	1.152	0.794
Hip fracture/dislocation	0.938	0.915	1.330**

Notes: * indicates statistically significant difference using negative binomial regression with $p<0.05$. **indicates statistically significant difference using negative binomial regression with $p<0.01$.

Source: falls_re_readmt_models.log, vcath_centered_xtmelogitJun20_2012.log, dvt_centered_xtmelogitJun20_2012.log.

3.3. The Excess Likelihood of Readmission Attributable to Three Hospital-Acquired Conditions

In ***Table 3-2***, we present our multivariate regression results on the excess likelihood of readmission attributable to three selected HACs. We generated the excess likelihood by using the results of the logistic models to estimate the likelihood of readmission assuming that all hospitalizations had an adverse event (HAC) and then to estimate the likelihood of readmission assuming that all hospitalizations had no adverse event (no HAC).

Table 3-2. Excess likelihood of readmission for selected hospital-acquired conditions

Hospital-acquired condition	Excess likelihood	Standard error
Falls and trauma	2.9%	0.5%
Vascular catheter-associated infection	5.6%	0.7%
DVT/PE following certain orthopedic procedures	1.8%	0.7%

Notes: DVT/PE = Deep vein thrombosis or pulmonary embolism.

Source: DVT_predicted.xlsx, Vcath_predicted.xlsx, fall_readmt_predict.log.

The difference between the two sets of predictions is the "excess" likelihood of readmission that can be attributed to the HAC after controlling for patient and hospital characteristics. We find that the falls and trauma HAC leads to an excess likelihood of readmission of 2.9 percentage points while the vascular catheter-associated infection HAC leads to an excess likelihood of readmission of 5.6 percentage points and the DVT/PE HAC leads to an excess likelihood of readmission of 1.8 percentage points. All of these results are statistically significant.

Section 4. Discharge to Post-Acute Care Settings

4.1. Descriptive Statistics on Discharge Destination

Table 4-1 presents descriptive statistics on the discharge destinations of patients in the HAC group and the comparison group. In the falls and trauma sample, 76.9% of the patients with the HAC were discharged to one of the PAC settings, while 57.4% of the patients in the control group were discharged to a PAC setting (statistically significant difference). On the other hand, patients with the HAC were significantly less likely to be discharged to home— 13.7% compared to 33.7% among the controls. There is no significant difference in the likelihood of discharge to other settings between those patients with the falls and trauma HAC and the comparison group.

Table 4-1. Discharge destination for selected hospital-acquired conditions

Hospital-acquired condition	HAC group	Comparison group	Difference
Falls and trauma			
Discharged to PAC setting	76.9%	57.4%	19.5%**
Discharged home	13.7%	33.7%	-20.0%**
Other	9.4%	8.9%	0.5%
Vascular catheter-associated infection			
Discharged to PAC setting	67.9%	53.2%	14.7%**
Discharged home	25.0%	24.9%	0.1%
Other	7.1%	21.9%	-14.8%**
DVT/PE following certain orthopedic procedures			
Discharged to PAC setting	88.0%	81.8%	6.2%**
Discharge home	8.5%	13.9%	-5.4%**
Other	3.5%	4.3%	-0.8%**

Notes: HAC = Hospital-acquired condition; PAC = Post-acute care; DVT/PE = Deep vein thrombosis or pulmonary embolism.

**indicates statistically significant difference using negative binomial regression with $p<0.01$. SOURCE: falls_pac_descriptive.log, vcath_pac_descriptive.log, dvt_pac_ descriptive.log.

In the vascular catheter-associated infection sample, 67.9% of the patients with the HAC were discharged to a PAC setting, compared with 53.2% of the patients in the control group (statistically significant difference) Patients with the HAC were discharged home at the same rate as patients in the control group, leaving a significant difference in the rate of discharge to other settings.

In the DVT/PE sample, there were significant differences between the HAC group and the comparison group for all discharge destinations, with the HAC group more likely to be discharged to a PAC setting (88.0% vs. 81.8%) and less likely to be discharged home (8.5% vs. 13.9%).

4.2. Relationship between Discharge Destination and the Likelihood of Readmission

Table 4-2 illustrates the relationship between the likelihood of readmission and whether the patient was discharged to a PAC setting for patients in the HAC and comparison groups. The results indicate that patients discharged to PAC settings are more likely to be readmitted within 30 days than those patients who were not discharged to PAC settings.

Table 4-2. Relationship between discharge to a post-acute care (PAC) setting and the likelihood of readmission for beneficiaries in the hospital-acquired condition and comparison groups

Hospital-acquired condition	Likelihood of readmission: HAC group	Likelihood of readmission: Comparison group
Falls and trauma		
Discharged to PAC setting	23.7%	19.8%
Not discharged to PAC	19.7%	14.5%
Vascular catheter-associated infection		
Discharged to PAC setting	32.0%	30.0%
Not discharged to PAC	28.0%	16.6%
DVT/PE following certain orthopedic procedures		
Discharged to PAC setting	12.8%	9.8%
Not discharged to PAC	6.8%	5.2%

Notes: HAC = Hospital-acquired condition; PAC = Post-acute care; DVT/PE = Deep vein thrombosis or pulmonary embolism.

**indicates statistically significant difference using negative binomial regression with $p<0.01$. SOURCE: falls_pac_descriptive.log, vcath_pac_descriptive.log, dvt_pac_descriptive.log.

4.3. Probability of Discharge to a Post-Acute Care Setting

We estimated a series of mixed effect logistic models to predict the probability of discharge to a PAC setting. As we did for readmissions, we estimated each of the three models described in ***Section 2.6*** for each of the HACs. Based on the results of these models, we present the results of Model II for falls and trauma and vascular catheter-associated infection. We do this, because the random effect on the HAC indicator is insignificant for each of these HACs. We present the results of Model III for the DVT/PE sample, due to the fact that the random effect on the HAC indicator is significant for this HAC. The model results are reported in ***Table 4-3***.

The main finding is that the presence of each HAC is associated with a greater likelihood of discharge to a PAC setting. The odds of being discharge to a PAC setting is 2.7 times greater for patients with the falls and trauma HAC, two times greater for patients with the vascular catheter-associated infection HAC, and 40% greater for patients with the DVT/PE HAC than for similar patients without the HACs.

Among the hospital-level covariates, we find that patients discharged from teaching hospitals are generally less likely to be discharged to a PAC setting, while patients from medium and large hospitals (those with at least 100 beds) are more likely to be discharged to a PAC setting than patients from smaller hospitals (those with fewer than 100 beds). Patients from urban hospitals are more likely to be discharged to a PAC setting than patients from rural hospitals.

Among the discharge-level covariates, we find that women are more likely to be discharged to a PAC setting than men and that there is a positive relationship between age and the likelihood of being discharged to a PAC setting. Medicaid enrollees are more likely to be discharged to PAC settings than non-enrollees, while patients who were initially eligible for Medicare due to disability are more likely to be discharged to a PAC setting than patients who became eligible due to age. Interestingly, patients with a history of ESRD are less likely to be discharged to a PAC setting, at least in two of the samples (falls and trauma and vascular catheter-associated infection), although these sample sizes are quite small, 126 and 316 in the HAC groups, respectively.

The results on the co-morbidity measures are mixed. Several of the measures that are significant are associated with a greater likelihood of PAC admission, but about half are associated with a smaller likelihood of PAC admission. It is likely that these co-morbidities are related to discharge to other inpatient settings that are not included in our PAC measure.

Table 4-3. Multivariate regression models for the likelihood of discharge to a post-acute care setting

Variable	Falls and trauma (n=78,827)	Vascular catheter-associated infection (n=44,981)	DVT/PE following certain orthopedic procedures (n=41,432)
HAC Indicator	**2.668****	**1.943****	**1.393****
Hospital-Level Covariates			
Urban	1.311**	1.390**	1.891**
Number of beds (reference is "fewer than 100"			
100-299	1.320**	1.093	2.226**
300 or more	1.297**	1.042	2.585**
Academic medical center	0.858**	0.894*	1.110
Discharge-Level Covariates			
Age (reference is "less than 65")			
65-74	1.570**	1.453**	1.363**
75-84	2.074**	1.925**	2.550**
85 and older	2.630**	1.968**	3.009**
Enrolled in Medicaid	1.175**	1.180**	1.199**
Original eligibility (reference is "aged")			
Disabled	1.107**	1.144**	1.351**
ESRD	0.711**	0.740**	1.625
Gender: Female	1.368**	1.145**	1.533**
Race (reference is "white")			
Black	1.229**	0.948	1.321**
Asian	0.584**	0.925	1.249
Other	1.011	0.809**	1.032
Institutionalized	1.333	0.881	0.293
Yale Comorbidity Measures			
Severe infection	0.907	0.962	1.141
Other infectious disease	1.220**	1.081	0.810
Metastatic cancer/acute leukemia	0.701**	0.618**	0.833
Severe cancer	0.702**	0.835**	0.840
Other major cancers	0.912**	1.102*	1.074
Diabetes mellitus	1.105**	1.098**	1.149**
Protein-calorie malnutrition	1.276**	1.173**	1.512
End-stage liver disease	0.932	0.844*	1.068
Other hematological disorders	0.825**	0.537**	2.084*
Drug and alcohol disorders	0.852*	0.870*	1.616
Psychiatric comorbidity	0.938	1.061	1.405*
Hemiplegia, paraplegia, paralysis and functional disability	1.310**	1.564**	1.093
Seizure disorders and convulsions	1.055	1.070	1.303
Congestive heart failure	0.913**	0.944*	0.907

Table 4-3. (Continued)

Variable	Falls and trauma (n=78,827)	Vascular catheter-associated infection (n=44,981)	DVT/PE following certain orthopedic procedures (n=41,432)
Coronary atherosclerosis or angina, cerebrovascular disease	0.956*	1.022	0.904
Specified arrhythmias	1.023	1.029	1.044
COPD	0.924**	1.026	1.237**
Dialysis status	0.796**	0.740**	0.756
Ulcers	1.682**	1.360**	1.039
Septicemia/shock	1.328**	1.227**	1.182
Cardio-respiratory failure and shock	1.064	1.173**	0.856
Acute renal failure	1.018	0.976	1.142
Pancreatic disease	0.751**	0.796**	0.947
Rheumatoid arthritis and inflammatory connective tissue disease	1.137**	0.961	1.230*
Respirator dependence	1.585**	1.333**	1.369
Transplants	0.916	0.740**	1.047
Hip fracture/dislocation	2.395**	1.527**	1.299*
NOTES:			

* indicates statistically significant difference using negative binomial regression with $p<0.05$. **indicates statistically significant difference using negative binomial regression with $p<0.01$. SOURCE: falls_pac_re_models.log, vcath_pac_re_models.log, DVT melogit Jun2012 Req2.log.

Section 5. Special Studies

5.1. Potential under-Coding of Hospital-Acquired Conditions

5.1.1. Introduction

In the Phase II report for this task, "Readmissions Due to Hospital-acquired Conditions (HACs)," we developed a mathematical model of readmission estimation bias that can occur when there is error in the measurement of hospital-acquired conditions, particularly when HACs are not reported. This can occur when clinical manifestation of the HAC occurs after the initial hospital discharge, such as for a SSI, or under-reporting by hospital staff. In this section, we focus on under-reporting of HACs on hospital claims, and in ***Section 5.2***, we look more closely at post-discharge presentation of

HAC-related conditions and post-discharge treatment that could be an indicator of a HAC-related condition.

The model demonstrates how one hospital can have a higher reported HAC rate if (a) it has more infections in general than average, and/or (b) if it has a higher likelihood of reporting its HACs. Conversely, a hospital with a lower-than-average HAC rate may truly have fewer HACs than other hospitals, or it may be under-reporting the incidence of HACs. Thus, two hospitals may have the same reported HAC rates but different readmission rates per admission leading to little correlation between the presence of a hospital-acquired condition and the likelihood of a readmission. It is also possible that one hospital has a lower reported HAC rate yet has a higher true infection readmission rate. The paradox is explained by the fact that the HAC rate calculated from claims data reflects two factors: the hospital's true, overall, HAC rate (once unreported, post-discharge, infections are accounted for) as well as the hospital's rate at which it reports HACs. The latter term may be both positive and negative; thus, an ambiguous net effect on the overall readmission rate. The reported or coded HAC rate can also vary positively or negatively with hospitals' overall infection rate. Thus, it is possible that a hospital has a high reported infection rate of all infections but a low readmission rate, thereby producing a zero correlation of reported HAC rates with readmission rates.

Model Implications

Conceptually, we would expect that the relationship between HAC rates and readmission rates to be positive; a HAC worsens a patient's health and could require multiple hospitalizations to treat. However, the "observed HAC" measure is imperfectly sensitive by failing to capture all true HACs. As a result, the observed relationship between HAC rates and readmission rates will not match the true relationship.

If the sensitivity is unrelated to the readmission rate and does not vary across providers, then this situation is analogous to the classic errors-in-variables regression problem, and the correlation between observed HAC rates and readmission rates will be lower than the true correlation. This biases the reported HAC coefficient in any readmission model towards zero, producing an under-estimate of the effect of true HACs on readmissions.

However, it is quite likely that the sensitivity of the observed HAC measure does vary systematically across providers (and type of HAC). To see this, consider two hospitals which differ only in their length of stay. One hospital tends to discharge patients as quickly as possible, whereas the second hospital tends to permit patients to stay in the hospital longer. In this hypothetical situation, we assume that the procedure infection rates and other aspects of underlying quality are identical but only the lengths of stay differ. In the early-discharge hospital, the infection may not be identified until after the patient is discharged. The inpatient HAC rate for this hospital will be low, but the readmission rate will be high. In contrast, in the second hospital, since the underlying length of stay is longer, the HAC may be identified and treated in the hospital prior to discharge (even further lengthening that patient's stay length). Assuming the patient is discharged with the HAC fully treated, no readmission would be necessary. Thus, the second hospital's reported inpatient HAC rate will be high, but its readmission rate will be low.

This confounding relationship between observed inpatient HAC rates and readmission rates is due to the fact that hospitals vary on two dimensions. First, hospitals vary in their true HAC rates because of differences in their quality of care. Second, hospitals will vary in their lengths of stay (or any other factor that would impair the sensitivity of the HAC measure). To counteract the confounding length of stay effect, one option must be to extend the time window for measuring (recording) HACs into the post-discharge period. Using readmissions to enhance the measure of true HAC rates can significantly improve the sensitivity of the initial HAC measure and produce a higher, more accurate estimate of the HAC-readmission link. Care must be taken, however, in inferring a HAC when using readmission data. Infections not acquired during the earlier admission will likely be picked up in using readmission data and make the measure somewhat less specific. Readmission data will also be imperfect to the extent that infections and other late-appearing HACs are treated in an ambulatory setting without a subsequent readmission. The modeling suggests taking a careful look at the complex relationship between a very imperfectly measured estimate of hospital-acquired conditions and any subsequent readmission rates. The shorter the window, the greater the likelihood that a HAC had gone unreported during the earlier hospitalization. It also calls for using non-readmission claims to track ambulatory follow-up of HACs (e.g., physician and outpatient department bills).

5.1.2. Data and Methods

From the twelve hospital-acquired conditions included in the HAC-POA payment policy, we selected seven for this analysis. Foreign object retained after surgery, air embolism, and blood incompatibility were excluded due to their relative infrequency in the hospital claims data. For the remaining HACs

– pressure ulcer stage III and IV, falls and trauma, catheter-associated urinary tract infection, vascular catheter-associated infection, manifestations of poor glycemic control, surgical site infections (included mediastinitis following CABG, SSI following certain orthopedic procedures, and SSI following bariatric surgery for obesity), and DVT/PE following certain orthopedic procedures – we constructed an episode of care file containing all IPPS hospitalizations in FY 2009 and FY 2010 with at least one of these conditions coded as hospital-acquired (POA indicator equal to "N" or "U"). In order to allow for a 30-day follow-up period after the initial (or "index") hospitalization, we excluded IPPS discharges that occurred on or after September 1, 2010 (approximately 4% of the initial sample).

For each of these HACs, we selected a comparison sample of IPPS hospitalizations that 1) did not have any of these HACs coded on the hospital claim, 2) did not have any of these HACrelated conditions coded as present on admission (POA indicators equal to "Y" or "W"), and 3) did not have any of these HAC-related diagnosis codes as the primary diagnosis on the claim. Since all hospital patients are potentially at risk for hospital-acquired pressure ulcer or falls and trauma, we selected a 5% sample of all of the claims that met the above criteria. To look for evidence of the manifestations of poor glycemic control HAC, we used a comparison group of 5% of IPPS claims that had a principal diagnosis of diabetes (ICD-9_CM diagnosis codes 250.00 – 250.99), since diabetic patients would be those at most at risk for poor glycemic control.

The remaining HACs, being specific to particular procedures or surgeries, had comparison groups selected based on the presence of ICD-9_CM procedure codes on the hospital claim. To check for under-coding of catheter-associated UTI, we selected all IPPS claims with a urinary catheter procedure code (57.94 or 57.95); note that this procedure code greatly under-estimates the actual rate of urinary catheters among hospital patients, as evidenced by the fact that only 5% of IPPS claims with a catheter-associated UTI have one of the urinary catheter procedure codes. We looked for evidence of vascular catheter-associated infections among a 25% sample of IPPS index claims that had a vascular catheter ICD-9_CM procedure code (38.93 or 38.95). For the three SSIs considered, we used the entire set of claims with the specified surgical procedures as our comparison sample, and for DVT/PE following certain orthopedic procedures, we took a 50% sample of all total hip replacement and total knee replacement surgeries to use for the population at risk for a DVT/PE. The sampling that we chose allowed us to significantly reduce computational time of these analyses while maintaining large enough comparison samples to find evidence of HAC under-coding. When presented in the following tables and descriptions, all samples have been adjusted to reflect 100% of the population; for example, any frequencies for the comparison sample of diabetic patients have been multiplied by 20 to reflect their size in the entire at-risk population in the FY 2009 and FY 2010 MedPAR files.

After selecting the IPPS index claims with HACs and the at-risk comparison samples for each of the HACs, we then used the unique beneficiary identifiers and admission and discharge dates on the index hospital claims to link physician claims that occurred during the index hospitalization to the hospital claim. Approximately 2% of index hospital claims had no linked physician claims. For index hospital claims that were linked to physician claims, we examined the reported diagnosis codes on both types of claims to look for evidence of HAC-related conditions.

We also looked forward 30 days from the hospital discharge date to identify any hospital readmissions that occurred for the beneficiaries in our sample, in order to examine readmission rates for those with and without hospital- and physician-identified HAC-related conditions. This analysis was limited to the hospital-acquired infections (catheter-associated UTI, vascular associated-catheter infections, and SSIs) and DVT/PE following certain orthopedic procedures.

For our analysis of post-discharge clinical presentation of infections and DVT/PE, we linked inpatient and outpatient Medicare claims – hospital, SNF, IRF, LTCH, outpatient, and physician claims – that occurred within 30 days of the index hospital discharge—and report frequency of post-discharge reporting of the HAC-related conditions and rates of readmission within 30 days. We restrict the reporting to only institutional claims. Using the outpatient claims, we further examined claims with HCPCS codes for antibiotic administration, to examine post-discharge treatment consistent with HAC-related infections.

5.1.3. Correlation between Hospital-Acquired Conditions Coded on Hospital Claims and Hospital-Acquired-Related Conditions Coded on Physician Claims

One way in which to determine the potential extent of under-coding of HACs on hospital claims is to compare the diagnosis codes on the hospital claims with the diagnosis codes on physician claims that were billed for the same patient during the hospitalization. In ***Table 5-1***, we show the frequencies of the HAC diagnosis codes on the hospital and the physician claims, for both the HAC populations and the at-risk comparison samples. In the first row, we present the number of index claims that had neither a hospital nor a physician diagnosis code of a HACrelated condition. The vast majority of claims in our analysis fall into this category. The second row shows, for each of the HACs in the analysis, the number of claims where the HAC is not coded on the index MedPAR hospital claim, but at least one physician claim linked to the index hospital claim has one of the HAC-related diagnosis codes. This is our set of potentially underreported HACs.

Some of these HAC-related conditions identified on the physician claims but not on the hospital claim may have actually been coded on the hospital claim, but not picked up by the MedPAR file and used for determining payment. Prior to January 2012, hospitals were not required to submit claims using the 5010 electronic format, which captures up to 24 secondary diagnosis codes. The older system captured only 8 secondary diagnosis codes. So while the HAC-related diagnosis code may have actually been reported on the hospital claim, for the purposes of analysis using pre-2012 hospital claims data, these HACs go unreported.

Appendix Table 4 provides some evidence that HAC diagnosis codes were reported after the eighth secondary diagnosis code on the hospital claims. In this table, we show the rates of HAC coding in FY 2010, when only the first 8 secondary diagnosis codes on the claim were recorded, compared to the rates of HAC coding in FY 2011 for those hospitals that began using the 5010 electronic format earlier than January 2012 and could report up to 24 secondary diagnosis codes. We found that hospitals using the 5010 electronic format represented about 94% of claims in FY 2011. As we would expect, for almost all of the HACs,[2] pressure ulcer stages III and IV, catheter associated urinary tract infection(CAUTI), vascular catheter associated infection (CLABSI), surgical site infections(SSIs), mediastinitis, following coronary artery bypass graft surgery, following certain orthopedic procedures, following bariatric surgery for obesity, and manifestations of poor glycemic control, the HAC rates increase when more diagnosis codes are used in the FY 2011 data. For example, see the Number of Discharges Identified as a HAC per Thousand for pressure ulcers stage III and IV. In FY 2010, there were 0.14 discharges per thousand with a pressure ulcer HAC, while in FY 2011, among the claims where up to 24 secondary diagnosis codes could be reported, the rate increased to 0.20. Therefore, some of the under-reporting we see in Table 5-1 is likely due to the limitation of 8 secondary diagnosis codes.

Additionally, some of these HAC-related conditions from the physician claims could have been present on admission; the large numbers of physician-identified falls and trauma and manifestations of poor glycemic control would seem to be more likely to reflect conditions that were present on admission rather than hospital-acquired. However, it seems less likely that the infections related to specific procedures or surgeries performed during the index hospitalization would be present on the admission before the procedure or surgery occurred, meaning that some of these physician-identified diagnoses could be truly un-reported HACs. For conditions such as mediastinitis following CABG, the 126 cases of mediastinitis identified only on the physician claims are likely to be true HACs. Regardless of the source of the under-reporting, the presence of true HACs among the hospital claims identified as not having HACs has the potential to bias our analysis of readmissions. While the numbers of physician-identified HAC-related conditions are generally small relative to the entire sample examined, they are often large relative to the number of HACs identified on the hospital claims. For example, from the set of orthopedic surgery claims that did not have a DVT/PE coded on the hospital claim (the first two rows in the table), only about 0.5% had a DVT/PE coded on a linked physician claim (3,622 out of 677,550). But when we compare that to the total number of DVT/PE HAC claims (the last two rows of the table) – 5,251 – it seems to be a much more significant number. If all of the physician-identified DVT/PE claims are true HACs, then the total count of DVT/PE HACs across the two years of data would be about 70% higher, 8,873 instead of 5,251. The physician claims for mediastinitis also point to potential under-reporting of HACs. From the MedPAR data, a total of 156,309 Medicare claims for CABG surgery were identified and linked to at least on physician claim during the period of hospitalization. Of those claims, 69 (.04%) had a diagnosis of mediastinitis on the hospital claim. In addition to these 69 hospital-reported mediastinitis HACs, there were 126 physician claims linked to hospital claims for CABG surgeries with a physician diagnosis code for mediastinitis. If all of these 126 physician-identified cases of mediastinitis were true HACs, then this data suggests that approximately 65% of mediastinitis HACs were unreported.[3]

The third row of the table counts the claims where the HAC diagnosis code was on the hospital claim but not on the physician claim, and the fourth row shows the claims where both hospital and physician claims report the HAC. The rate of agreement between hospital and physician coding of these HACs is poor. Except for falls and trauma and DVT/PE following certain orthopedic procedures, there are more hospital-identified HACs without an accompanying physician diagnosis of the HAC than there are claims with both hospital and physician claims report the HAC.

It would appear that neither hospital claims nor physician claims are fully coding all of the HACs that are occurring in the hospital.

5.1.4. Under-Coding of Hospital-Acquired Conditions and the Effect on Readmission Rates

Having identified a set of potentially under-coded HACs, we now examine how these under-coded HACs could affect measures of readmission rates. In ***Tables 5-2a*** through ***5-2c***, we present the 7-day, 15-day, and 30-day all-cause readmission rates for hospital claims with and without HACs, linked to physician claims with and without the HAC-related diagnosis codes. The rates presented calculate the number of discharges per 100 discharges that had at least one hospital readmission within the specified window. We limit this analysis of readmission rates to catheter-associated urinary tract infections, vascular catheter-associated infections, the three subsets of SSIs, and DVT/PE following certain orthopedic procedures.

For four of the HACs in the 7-day readmission window, and for all of the HACs in the 15-day and 30-day readmission windows, the lowest readmission rates are seen for the claims with neither a hospital- nor a physician-identified a HAC-related condition. When considering discharges with a physician-identified (but no hospital-identified) HAC-related condition, the second row in each series of 4 rows, the readmission rates are typically more similar to those of the hospital-identified HACs than to those with no HAC-related diagnoses. For example, consider the final column where we report the readmission rates for claims with certain orthopedic procedures (total hip replacement and total knee replacement), with and without a diagnosis of a DVT/PE.

The readmission rate within 7 days is 3.3 per 100 discharges for surgical patients with no DVT/PE-related diagnosis code, 9.2 per 100 discharges for those with DVT/PE diagnosis code reported on the physician claim only, 7.2 per 100 discharges for those with DVT/PE diagnosis code reported on the hospital claim only, and 7.1 per 100 discharges for those with both a hospital and physician reported DVT/PE. The readmission rate for orthopedic surgery patients with no DVT/PE diagnosis is half or less than half of the readmission rate for patients with a DVT/PE diagnosis, regardless of whether the DVT/PE is coded on the physician claim or the hospital claim or both.

Table 5-1. Frequency of hospital and physician coding of selected hospital-acquired conditions

Hospital Diagnosis of HAC	Physician Diagnosis of HAC	Pressure Ulcer – Stages III & IV[1]	Falls and Trauma[2]	Catheter-Associated Urinary Tract Infection (CAUTI)[3]	Vascular Catheter - Associated Infection (CLABSI)[4]	Manifestation of Poor Glycemic Control[5]	Surgical Site Infection (SSI), Mediastinitis following Coronary Artery Bypass Graft (CABG)[6]	Surgical Site Infection (SSI) following Certain Orthopedic Procedures[7]	Surgical Site Infection Following Bariatric Surgery for Obesity[8]	Deep Vein Thrombosis or Pulmonary Embolism (DVT/PE) Following Certain Orthopedic Procedures[9]
No	No	17,742,320	17,392,660	151,795	1,365,324	4,683,940	156,114	203,780	29,679	673,928
No	Yes	1,720	35,380	117	4,148	14,340	126	849	163	3,622
Yes	No	2,508	3,103	6,175	6,534	655	41	227	24	1,511
Yes	Yes	60	7,064	81	488	226	28	151	8	3,740
	Total	17,746,608	17,754,207	158,168	1,376,494	4,699,161	156,309	205,007	29,874	682,801

Notes:

[1] 2.6% of MedPAR index admissions with no hospital diagnosis of pressure ulcer, and 2.2% of admissions with a pressure ulcer HAC, were excluded because they had no linked physician claims during the hospitalization period. 5% sample of hospital claims without the HAC multiplied by 20 to estimate the full population.

[2] Includes fracture, dislocation, intracranial injury, crushing injury, burn, and other injuries. 2.6% of MedPAR index admissions with no hospital diagnosis of falls and trauma, and 2.0% of admissions with a falls and trauma HAC, were excluded because they had no linked physician claims during the hospitalization period. 5% sample of hospital claims without the HAC multiplied by 20 to estimate the full population.

[3] 2.4% of MedPAR index admissions with no hospital diagnosis of CAUTI, and 2.0% of admissions with a CAUTI HAC, were excluded because they had no linked physician claims during the hospitalization period.

[4] 2.0% of MedPAR index admissions with no hospital diagnosis of CLABSI, and 2.4% of admissions with a CLABSI HAC, were excluded because they had no linked physician claims during the hospitalization period. 25% sample of hospital claims with vascular catheter procedure without the HAC multiplied by 4 to estimate the full population.

[5] Includes diabetic ketoacidosis, nonketotic hyperosmolar coma, hypoglycemic coma, secondary diabetes with ketoacidosis, and secondary diabetes with hyperosmolarity. 2.6% of MedPAR index admissions with no hospital diagnosis of poor glycemic control, and 2.8% of admissions with a poor glycemic control HAC, were excluded because they had no linked physician claims during the hospitalization period. 5% sample of hospital claims with diabetes without the HAC multiplied by 20 to estimate the full population.

[6] 0.2% of MedPAR index admissions with no hospital diagnosis of mediastinitis, and 0.2% of admissions with a mediastinitis HAC, were excluded because they had no linked physician claims during the hospitalization period.

[7] Includes spine, neck, shoulder, and elbow surgeries. 2.4% of MedPAR index admissions with no hospital diagnosis of SSI, and 4.5% of admissions with an SSI following certain orthopedic procedures HAC, were excluded because they had no linked physician claims during the hospitalization period.

[8] Includes laparoscopic gastric bypass, gastroenterostomy, and laparoscopic gastric restrictive surgery. 2.4% of MedPAR index admissions with no hospital diagnosis of SSI, and 5.9% of admissions with an SSI following bariatric surgery HAC, were excluded because they had no linked physician claims during the hospitalization period.

[9] Includes total hip replacement and total knee replacement. 2.2% of MedPAR index admissions with no hospital diagnosis of DVT/PE, and 2.3% of admissions with a DVT/PE HAC, were excluded because they had no linked physician claims during the hospitalization period. 50% sample of orthopedic procedures without the DVT HAC multiplied by 2 to estimate the full population.

Source: MedPAR hospital claims from FY 2009 and the first eleven months of FY 2010 linked to Medicare Part B physician claims during the hospitalization.

Table 5-2a. Readmission rates per 100 discharges for 7-day readmission window for selected hospital-acquired conditions (HACs) identified from hospital and or physician claims and for comparisons with discharges with no reported HAC

Hospital Diagnosis of HAC	Physician Diagnosis of HAC	Catheter-Associated Urinary Tract Infection (CAUTI)[3]	Vascular Catheter -Associated Infection (CLABSI)[4]	Surgical Site Infection (SSI), Mediastinitis following Coronary Artery Bypass Graft (CABG)[6]	Surgical Site Infection (SSI) following Certain Orthopedic Procedures[7]	Surgical Site Infection Following Bariatric Surgery for Obesity[8]	Deep Vein Thrombosis and Pulmonary Embolism (DVT/PE) Following Certain Orthopedic Procedures[9]
No	No	9.0	10.3	8.5	4.0	5.3	3.3
No	Yes	7.7	12.4	15.9	9.9	14.7	9.2
Yes	No	9.1	12.4	14.6	9.3	4.2	7.2
Yes	Yes	11.1	13.5	11.1	7.3	12.5	7.1

Table 5-2b. Readmission rates per 100 discharges for 15-day readmission window for selected hospital-acquired conditions (HACs) identified from hospital and or physician claims and for comparisons with discharges with no reported HAC

Hospital Diagnosis of HAC	Physician Diagnosis of HAC	Catheter-Associated Urinary Tract Infection (CAUTI)[3]	Vascular Catheter-Associated Infection (CLABSI)[4]	Surgical Site Infection (SSI), Mediastinitis following Coronary Artery Bypass Graft (CABG)[6]	Surgical Site Infection (SSI) following Certain Orthopedic Procedures[7]	Surgical Site Infection Following Bariatric Surgery for Obesity[8]	Deep Vein Thrombosis and Pulmonary Embolism (DVT/PE) Following Certain Orthopedic Procedures[9]
No	No	14.7	16.8	13.6	6.7	8.2	4.9
No	Yes	17.1	22.5	22.2	17.7	21.5	12.3
Yes	No	15.8	20.8	22.0	13.7	12.5	9.9
Yes	Yes	16.0	22.5	18.5	11.9	25.0	10.6

Table 5-2c. Readmission rates per 100 discharges for 30-day readmission window for selected hospital-acquired conditions (HACs) identified from hospital and or physician claims and for comparisons with discharges with no reported HAC

Hospital Diagnosis of HAC	Physician Diagnosis of HAC	Catheter-Associated Urinary Tract Infection (CAUTI)[3]	Vascular Catheter -Associated Infection (CLABSI)[4]	Surgical Site Infection (SSI), Mediastinitis following Coronary Artery Bypass Graft (CABG)[6]	Surgical Site Infection (SSI) following Certain Orthopedic Procedures[7]	Surgical Site Infection Following Bariatric Surgery for Obesity[8]	Deep Vein Thrombosis and Pulmonary Embolism (DVT/PE) Following Certain Orthopedic Procedures[9]
No	No	21.7	24.8	18.9	9.6	11.6	6.9
No	Yes	28.2	33.2	28.6	24.7	30.1	15.6
Yes	No	24.2	30.0	34.1	22.0	20.8	13.2
Yes	Yes	18.5	34.4	29.6	22.5	37.5	14.5

Notes: See Table 5-1 for frequencies for each cell, and see notes on Table 5-1 for further details on the sample

Source: MedPAR hospital claims from FY 2009 and the first eleven months of FY 2010 linked to Medicare Part B physician claims during the hospitalization and linked to MedPAR inpatient claims up to 30 days after the hospital discharge.

5.2. Timing to Clinical Presentation of Selected Conditions

5.2.1. Time to Physician Diagnosis of Conditions During Hospitalization

For catheter-associated urinary tract infections, vascular catheter-associated infections, SSIs, and DVT/PE following certain orthopedic procedures that were identified on physician claims linked to the hospital claim, we looked at the dates of the relevant procedures on the hospital claim and compared them to the dates on the first physician claim with a HAC-related diagnosis, to show the amount of time that passes between the procedure and the HAC-related condition. We combined data from the physician-identified HAC-related conditions that were identified as HACs on the hospital claim with those who were not identified as HACs on the hospital claim, such that the sample sums the second and fourth rows of Table 5-1. In ***Table 5-3***, we report the time to a physician diagnosis of a HAC-related condition.

In the second row, we report the number and percent of hospitalizations (for HACs and those at risk for HACs who had a physician diagnosis of the HAC-related condition) where the physician diagnosis code of the HAC-related conditions occurred prior to the catheter insertion or surgery data. These diagnoses occurring prior to procedure could be error in coding, either of the diagnosis or procedure dates, or they could also represent conditions that were POA. CAUTI and CLABSI are more likely to occur before the procedure date, with 22.5% of physician-identified CAUTI diagnoses, and 45.9% of physician-identified CLABSI diagnoses, occurring prior to the hospital procedure date for the catheter insertion. This could be caused by a catheter being replaced (and coded) after the discovery of the infection.

Time to physician diagnosis of CAUTI and DVT/PE following certain orthopedic procedures is typically much faster than the timing to the other HAC-related infections. For CAUTI, 60% of physician-identified cases occur within 3 days of the catheter insertion procedure, and 77.5% of DVT/PE cases diagnosed by a physician occur within 3 days of the orthopedic surgery. In contrast, more than half of two of the SSIs are first diagnosed more than a week after the relevant surgical procedures. For example, for all cases of mediastinitis following CABG surgery identified on a physician claim, 35.7 % were first diagnosed between 8 and 15 days after the surgery and 44.8 % were first diagnosed 16 or more days after the surgery.

Table 5-3. Time to presentation of selected conditions from physician claims during initial hospitalization, all claims with a physician diagnosis of selected hospital-acquired conditions

Time to Presentation	Catheter-Associated Urinary Tract Infection (CAUTI)	Vascular Catheter-Associated Infection (CLABSI)	Surgical Site Infection (SSI), Mediastinitis following Coronary Artery Bypass Graft (CABG)	Surgical Site Infection (SSI) following Certain Orthopedic Procedures	Surgical Site Infection Following Bariatric Surgery for Obesity	Deep Vein Thrombosis or Pulmonary Embolism (DVT/PE) Following Certain Orthopedic Procedures
Hospital claim with procedure linked to physician claim with						
HAC diagnosis codes						
Freq.	120	4,442	154	1,000	171	7,362
Percent	100.0%	100.0%	100.0%	100.0%	100.0%	100.0%
Physician diagnosis of HAC-related condition prior to date of procedure						
Freq.	27	2,039	12	72	21	292
Percent	22.5%	45.9%	7.8%	7.2%	12.3%	4.0%
Physician diagnosis of HAC-related condition 0 to 3 days after procedure						
Freq.	72	1,469	8	400	33	5,708
Percent	60.0%	33.1%	5.2%	40.0%	19.3%	77.5%
Physician diagnosis of HAC-related condition between 4 and						
7 days after procedure						
Freq.	9	334	10	219	24	1,160
Percent	7.5%	7.5%	6.5%	21.9%	13.8%	15.8%
Physician diagnosis of HAC-related condition between 8 and						

Time to Presentation	Catheter-Associated Urinary Tract Infection (CAUTI)	Vascular Catheter-Associated Infection (CLABSI)	Surgical Site Infection (SSI), Mediastinitis following Coronary Artery Bypass Graft (CABG)	Surgical Site Infection (SSI) following Certain Orthopedic Procedures	Surgical Site Infection Following Bariatric Surgery for Obesity	Deep Vein Thrombosis or Pulmonary Embolism (DVT/PE) Following Certain Orthopedic Procedures
15 days after procedure						
Freq.	10	332	55	207	63	168
Percent	8.3%	7.5%	35.7%	20.7%	36.8%	2.3%
Physician diagnosis of HAC-related condition between 16 days or more after procedure						
Freq.	2	268	69	102	30	34
Percent	1.7%	6.0%	44.8%	10.2%	17.5%	0.5%

Notes:

[1] Excludes 78 CAUTI HAC claims that did not have a urinary catheter procedure coded.

[2] Excludes 194 CLABSI HAC claims that did not have a vascular catheter procedure coded. See notes on Table 5-1 for further details on the sample

Source: MedPAR hospital claims from FY 2009 and the first eleven months of FY 2010 linked to Medicare Part B physician claims during the hospitalization.

Table 5-4. Physician specialty from the first diagnosis of HAC-related condition, among all hospital claims linked to a physician claim with a HAC-related diagnosis code

Physician Specialty	Catheter-Associated Urinary Tract Infection (CAUTI)	Vascular Catheter-Associated Infection (CLABSI)	Surgical Site Infection (SSI), Mediastinitis following Coronary Artery Bypass Graft (CABG)	Surgical Site Infection (SSI) following Certain Orthopedic Procedures	Surgical Site Infection Following Bariatric Surgery for Obesity	Deep Vein Thrombosis or Pulmonary Embolism (DVT/PE) Following Certain Orthopedic Procedures
Number of physician-identified HAC-related diagnosis linked to hospital claim	198	4,636	154	1,000	171	7,362
Most common physician specialty (Percent)	Infectious disease specialist (31%)	Infectious disease specialist (21%)	Infection disease specialist (24%)	Infectious disease specialist (24%)	General surgery (21%)	Diagnostic radiology (46%)
Second most common physician specialty (Percent)	Ambulance service supplier (22%)	Diagnostic radiology (15%)	Plastic surgeons (14%)	Anesthesiology (22%)	Diagnostic radiology (19%)	Internal medicine (19%)
Third most common physician specialty (Percent)	Internal medicine (17%)	Internal medicine (14%)	Internal medicine specialists (12%)	Orthopedic surgery (15%)	Infectious disease specialist (18%)	Vascular surgery (6%)
Fourth most common physician specialty (Percent)	Urology (7%)	General surgery (13%)	Cardiac surgeons (9%)	Neurosurgery (9%)	Anesthesiology (11%)	Pulmonary disease (5%)
Fifth most common physician specialty (Percent)	Diagnostic radiology (5%)	Anesthesiology (8%)	Thoracic surgeons (8%)	Internal medicine (6%)	CRNA (7%)	Cardiology (5%)

Notes: See notes on Table 5-1 for further details on the sample

Source: MedPAR hospital claims from FY 2009 and the first eleven months of FY 2010 linked to Medicare Part B physician claims during the hospitalization.

We also examined the physician specialty type for patients who had a physician-identified HAC-related condition, whether or not the HAC was coded on the hospital claims, to see what physician specialties might be potential indicators for the HAC-related conditions. In ***Table 5-4***, we present the top five physician specialties for the first physician claim linked to the hospital claim with a HAC-related diagnosis code.

Infectious disease specialists were the most likely type of physician to make the initial diagnosis of the HAC-related condition for four of the five infection conditions (CAUTI, CLABSI, mediastinitis following CABG, and SSI following certain orthopedic procedures), accounting for more than 20% of initial diagnoses for these conditions. For SSI following bariatric procedures, infectious disease specialists first diagnosed 18% of HAC-related conditions. Internal medicine physician are often the first to diagnose many of the HAC-related conditions. Urologists are among the top 5 physician types for diagnosing CAUTI, and orthopedic surgeons are the third common physician specialty to diagnose an SSI following certain orthopedic procedures. Interestingly, 22% of CAUTI conditions are diagnosed by ambulance service suppliers. Recall from Table 5-3 that just over 22% of CAUTI diagnoses on the physician claims occur before the date of the insertion of a urinary catheter on the hospital claim.

It is likely, then, that these infections identified by ambulance service suppliers occurred in another healthcare setting (or at home) and are coded during ambulance transfer to the hospital.

For those beneficiaries who had a DVT/PE coded on the physician claims linked to a hospital claim for certain orthopedic surgeries, the most common first physician specialty type coded was diagnostic radiology (46%), followed by internal medicine (19%), vascular surgery (6%), pulmonary disease (5%), and cardiology (5%). It is not surprising that diagnostic radiology was the most frequently coded first physician specialty and internal medicine was the next most common physician specialty as patients are referred to diagnostic radiology for testing to confirm the presence or absence of a DVT or PE, often by an internal medicine physician's assessment of a possible DVT or PE.

5.2.2. Post-Discharge Diagnosis of Conditions in Inpatient Settings

In ***Table 5-5***, we consider the sample of index claims that had neither a hospital- nor a physician-identified hospital-acquired condition, and we look for subsequent inpatient claims with diagnosis codes that are used to identify hospital-acquired conditions. We do not include any of the follow-up hospital claims where the relevant diagnosis codes are identified as being hospital-acquired (POA indicator equal to "N" or "U"), since we are looking specifically for evidence of the conditions that stem from the procedure or surgery in the index hospital claim. We also do not include any of the conditions that can occur due to poor care in any inpatient setting (pressure ulcer stages III or IV, falls and trauma, and manifestations of poor glycemic control). The number and percent of inpatient claims (hospital, SNF, LTCH, IRF, and other inpatient claims) within the 7-day, 15-day, and 30-day window following the index hospital discharge that have the relevant diagnosis codes for each group are presented. Note that we do not refer to these as hospital-acquired conditions, because the first evidence from the claims data that these conditions occurred comes after the index hospital discharge, and thus we cannot determine if the conditions were actually acquired in the index hospitalization. Instead, we use the term "HAC-related" to refer to diagnosis codes/conditions that are considered HACs when they are coded as not present on admission (POA indicator equal to "N" or "U") in an IPPS hospital, but can present themselves in any health care setting. Some of these may have been uncoded HACs in the index hospital setting, but many may be HAC-related conditions whose clinical presentation did not occur until after the index discharge. As we saw in Table 5-3, the time to presentation for many of these HAC-related conditions, particularly the surgical site infections, can be more than 1 or 2 weeks. Short hospital stays increase the likelihood that an infection will not clinically present and be reported until after the initial hospital discharge. Within the 7-day follow-up window, about half of the claims identified with a HACrelated condition are readmissions to a hospital, which illustrates the strong relationship between post-discharge presentation of these conditions and hospital readmissions. Although a readmission to a hospital is the primary source of post-discharge diagnosis of these HAC-related conditions overall, DVT/PE is more likely to be found on a SNF claim and vascular catheter-associated infection is more likely to be found on an LTCH claim. Even though the rates of these conditions are fairly low within our samples, the frequencies are often sizable relative to the number of hospital- and physician-identified conditions. For example, among SSI following certain orthopedic procedures, there were 1,620 cases of surgical site infections identified on inpatient claims that occurred within 7 days of the discharge from the index hospital claim where the surgery was performed, compared to 378 infections identified on the hospital claims and 849 infections identified on the physician claims only (see Table 5-1).

Table 5-5. Time to presentation of selected conditions on inpatient claims following index hospital discharge with no hospital or physician diagnosis of selected hospital-acquired conditions

Time to Presentation	Catheter-Associated Urinary Tract Infection (CAUTI)	Vascular Catheter-Associated Infection (CLABSI)	Surgical Site Infection (SSI), Mediastinitis following Coronary Artery Eypass Graft (CABG)	Surgical Site Infection (SSI) following Certain Orthopedic Procedures	Surgical Site Infection Following Bariatric Surgery for Obesity	Deep Vein Thrombosis or Pulmonary Embolism (DVT/PE) Following Certain Orthopedic Procedures
Index hospital claim with procedure code, without HAC diagnosis codes, and linked to physician claims without HAC diagnosis codes						
Freq.	151,795	1,365,324	156,114	203,780	29,679	673,928
Percent	100%	100%	100%	100%	100%	100%
7-day window: any inpatient claim with HAC-related diagnosis codes						
Freq.	230	5,728	132	1,620	243	4,314
Percent	0.2%	0.4%	0.1%	0.8%	0.8%	0.6%
15-day window: any inpatient claim with HAC-related diagnosis codes						
Freq.	436	8,088	238	2,942	364	5,404
Percent	0.3%	0.6%	0.2%	1.4%	1.2%	0.8%
30-day window: any inpatient claim with HAC-related diagnosis codes						
Freq.	715	11,504	329	4,062	465	6,718
Percent	0.5%	0.8%	0.2%	2.0%	1.6%	1.0%

Notes: See notes on Table 5-1 for further details on the sample

Source: MedPAR hospital claims from FY 2009 and the first eleven months of FY 2010 linked to Medicare Part B physician claims during the hospitalization and linked to MedPAR inpatient claims up to 30 days after the hospital discharge.

Table 5-6. Outpatient department (OPD) drug claims within 30 days of hospital discharge, for patients with and without a HAC

OPD Drug Claims	Catheter-Associated Urinary Tract Infection (CAUTI): HAC group	Catheter-Associated Urinary Tract Infection (CAUTI): At-risk group	Surgical Site Infection (SSI), Mediastinitis following Coronary Artery Bypass Graft (CABG): HAC group	Surgical Site Infection (SSI), Mediastinitis following Coronary Artery Bypass Graft (CABG): At-risk group	Surgical Site Infection (SSI) following Certain Orthopedic Procedures: HAC group	Surgical Site Infection (SSI) following Certain Orthopedic Procedures: At-risk group	Surgical Site Infection Following Bariatric Surgery for Obesity: HAC group	Surgical Site Infection Following Bariatric Surgery for Obesity: At-risk group
Total of hospital claims	6,382	155,726	71	156,612	396	209,569	34	30,573
Number with 30-day post-discharge OPD drug claim for antibiotic treatment	124	3,500	2	2,401	16	2,143	0	513
Percent with 30-day post-discharge OPD drug claim for antibiotic treatment	1.9%	2.2%	2.8%	1.5%	4.0%	1.0%	0%	1.7%
Most frequently observed	Cefazolin/	Vancomycin/	Daptomycin/	Vancomycin/	Daptomycin/	Vancomycin/	N/A	Cefazolin/
OPD drugs/ Percent of	28.6%	26.1%	93.3%	37.4%	41.4%	31.5%		19.63%
most frequently observed	Vancomycin/	Ceftriaxone/	Cefazolin/	Daptomycin/	Vancomycin/	Daptomycin/		Vancomycin/
OPD drugs	25%	16.2%	6.7%	10.7%	26.7%	21.3%		15.5%
	Levofloxacin/	Cefazolin/		Ceftriaxone/	Ertapenem/	Ceftriaxone/		Unclassified
	21.4%	12.5%		10.1%	15.2%	16.5%		Drugs/ 13.9%
	Unclassified	Gentamicin/		Cefazolin/		Cefazolin/		Ertapenem/
	drugs/10.7%	8.0%		8.9%		8.2%		10.7%

OPD Drug Claims	Catheter-Associated Urinary Tract Infection (CAUTI): HAC group	Catheter-Associated Urinary Tract Infection (CAUTI): At-risk group	Surgical Site Infection (SSI), Mediastinitis following Coronary Artery Bypass Graft (CABG): HAC group	Surgical Site Infection (SSI), Mediastinitis following Coronary Artery Bypass Graft (CABG): At-risk group	Surgical Site Infection (SSI) following Certain Orthopedic Procedures: HAC group	Surgical Site Infection (SSI) following Certain Orthopedic Procedures: At-risk group	Surgical Site Infection Following Bariatric Surgery for Obesity: HAC group	Surgical Site Infection Following Bariatric Surgery for Obesity: At-risk group
	Ceftriaxone/	Levofloxacin/				Ertapenem/		Ceftriaxone/
	3.6%	7.9%				4.7%		10.3%
		Unclassified						
		Drugs/ 7.2%						

Source: MedPAR hospital claims from FY 2009 and the first eleven months of FY 2010 linked to Medicare OPD drug claims up to 30 days after the hospital discharge.

As these are cumulative frequencies and rates, the numbers of these conditions identified on inpatient claims increases as the follow-up window increases. Hospital readmissions are responsible for an even larger percentage of these HAC-related diagnoses in the 15-day window, around two thirds of the total, with other post-acute settings playing a less prominent role. After hospitals, vascular catheter-associated infections, mediastinitis following CABG, and SSI following bariatric surgery are most likely to be diagnosed in an LTCH, while SSI following orthopedic surgery is most likely to be diagnosed in an IRF and DVT/PE following certain orthopedic procedures is most likely to be diagnosed in a SNF.

At the 30-day window, there are more of HAC-related conditions diagnosed on the follow-up inpatient claims than on the index hospital claims alone, except for catheter-associated UTI; with the further exception of DVT/PE following certain orthopedic procedures, there are more of these conditions diagnosed on the follow-up claims than on index hospital and physician claims combined. While these may or may not have been true HACs, the presence of these conditions post-discharge is leading to more readmissions and resource use.

5.3. Post-Discharge Use of Outpatient Department Drugs for Infection Treatment

In this portion of the analysis, we used outpatient department (OPD) drug claims in the 30 days after a hospital discharge to examine post-discharge treatment consistent with HACrelated infections. We looked at four HAC-related conditions – CAUTI, SSI-mediastinitis after CABG surgery, SSI following bariatric surgery, and SSI following certain orthopedic procedures – to identify potential under-reporting of these conditions during the hospital period or clinical presentation of infections after discharge. As with the previous analyses, our initial sample contained all IPPS claims with one of these four HACs, and also those beneficiaries who did not have a reported HAC on their hospital claims, but who were identified as being at risk for a HAC due to the surgery (CABG, bariatric surgery, or orthopedic surgery) or procedure (placement of urinary catheter) that was performed during the index hospitalization. Our population of interest was the sample of beneficiaries who had at least one OPD drug claim that contained one of the Healthcare Common Procedure Coding System (HCPCS) procedure codes for antibiotics known to treat these infections.

We identified specific medications used to treat the HAC-related infections a priori through peer-reviewed literature, drug-related websites, drug reference books, and limited validation with physicians. We also identified the drugs that were used in the OPD data to treat beneficiaries with a reported HAC and compared them to the a priori list of antibiotics to ensure that these medications were included in our analysis. It should be noted that the HCPCS antibiotic codes included in this analysis are specific to antibiotics that are administered intramuscularly or intravenously. The OPD file provides a count of the number of occurrences of the antibiotic HCPCS codes at the revenue center on a claim. This means that an individual beneficiary may have multiple OPD drug claims for a specific antibiotic treatment plan that includes one or more administrations within the 30 day period. The outcome of interest in our analysis is the presence of at least one OPD drug claim for one of the specified antibiotics. In this section of the report, we present a summary of our findings for all of the four studied HACs.

In *Table 5-6*, we present a summary of OPD drug claims 30 days after hospital discharge, for beneficiaries with and without one of the studied HACs. The first row gives the total number of hospital discharges with the HAC or at risk for the HAC. The second and third rows report the number and percent of hospital discharges with a 30-day post-discharge OPD drug claim for antibiotic treatment. The fourth row reports the most frequently administered OPD antibiotics and the percent of the total among those with OPD antibiotics.

Using mediastinitis following CABG as an example, there are a total of 156,612 discharges with CABG procedures (ICD-9_CM procedure codes 36.10-36.19) without a diagnosis code for mediastinitis on the hospital claim, and 71 discharges with CABG procedures and a hospital-acquired diagnosis of mediastinitis. Among the 156,612 discharges without a reported HAC that were at risk for mediastinitis, there are 2,401 discharges (1.5%) with OPD antibiotic drug claims appropriate for the treatment of mediastinitis. The ratio of at-risk discharges with an OPD antibiotic drug claim to reported hospital-based mediastinitis discharges is 34-to-1.

There are at least five potential reasons 2,401 CABG patients are reporting anti-infective drug use within 30 days after discharge. First, some patients may have already had an infection of another origin when admitted for the procedure and so are continuing antibiotic treatment after discharge. Second, some patients may have been infected after discharge from poor adherence to post-discharge instructions. Third, some patients could have been treated for a post-discharge infection unrelated to the surgery. Fourth, patients may have contracted a sternal wound infection that advanced to mediastinitis post-discharge. And fifth, the hospital might not have reported a mediastinitis infection during the CABG hospitalization.

The most frequently observed OPD antibiotic drugs across these four HACs are similar between both the reported and at-risk groups for each of the conditions as well as across all four HACs. This is most likely attributed to the bacterial origin of the infection and the specific antimicrobial therapy as all of these HACs have either a surgical or invasive procedure component that places patients at higher risk for an infection. For example, vancomycin, a glycopeptides antibiotic used for prophylaxis as well as treatment of infections caused by Gram-positive bacteria, is observed in all four at-risk groups and two of the three HAC groups with OPD antibiotic drug claims. (There are no observed OPD antibiotic drug claims for the 34 reported SSIs following bariatric surgery.) Gram-positive bacteria include such organisms as *Staphylococcus aureus* and *Staphylococcus epidermis*. Vancomycin is also used in the treatment of methicillin-resistant *S. aureus* (MRSA) infections that are resistant to other antibiotics. The use of vancomycin across all HACs is highest among the CABG patients who are at risk for mediastinitis (37.4% of those with OPD antibiotics received vancomycin) and lowest in the at-risk group for SSIs following bariatric surgery (15.5%). Daptomycin, a newer Gram-positive antibiotic, is used to treat skin and soft tissue infections as well as MRSA. Daptomycin claims are present in both the reported and at-risk groups for mediastinitis and SSIs following orthopedic surgery. Prescriptions for Daptomycin were not observed in OPD drug claims for SSI following bariatric surgery nor CAUTI. Clinical trials are ongoing to test the efficacy of Daptomycin in treating urinary tract infections.

When combined there are a total of 553,319 discharges used in this analysis, with only 6,883 reported HACs. Among the 552,480 discharges that are at risk but without a reported HAC, there are 8,557 discharges with one or more OPD drug claims for antibiotics appropriate for treatment of one or more of the hospital-acquired conditions. Some of these 8,557 discharges could potentially have been true HACs that were not reported by the hospital.

We observed diverse rates of potentially unreported HACs based on outpatient drug claims for CAUTI and SSIs for orthopedic, bariatric surgery, and CABG. The ratio of at-risk patient with outpatient antibiotic treatment to reported HACs ranged from .55-to-1 for CAUTI to 34-to-1 for mediastinitis following CABG. Among the studied conditions, CAUTI had the highest number of discharges with the HAC (6,382) as compared to the other three HACs. The at-risk group for CAUTI had 3,500 discharges with an OPD antibiotic claim, which was higher both in frequency terms and in percentage terms than the other three HACs. This difference may be attributed to the fact that patients with urinary catheters are at higher risk for infection due to the hospital environment and their own co-morbidities. Another explanation may be that CAUTI infections are more readily identified when they do occur in the hospital due to the recent national attention and success in implementing evidence –based procedures to prevent urinary catheter infections. Or, they manifest clinically earlier than other infections, as we saw in Table 5-3.

There are a number of limitations to using drug data to identify potentially unreported healthcare-acquired infections. One is that many of the drugs used to treat a specific HAC, such as mediastinitis, are also used to treat other infections. For instance Cefazolin may be used to treat infections related to CABG surgery, but it is also used to treat the other three HACs, as observed in our analysis. Antibiotics are prescribed based on the presenting bacterial pathogen and the results of bacterial blood cultures and drug sensitivity testing rather than the specific condition. A beneficiary with mediastinitis may present with the pathogen staphylococcus aureus and be treated with a specific antibiotic for that pathogen and a different drug, like daptomycin for a more serious infection like MRSA. Third, beneficiaries may have more than one site at risk for infection. For example, a beneficiary undergoing a CABG procedure is at risk for both a sternal infection, mediastinitis, as well as an infection at the surgical site where the vein was harvested for the bypass graft (saphenous or internal mammary artery); these infections may be treated with different antibiotics depending on the presenting pathogen.

OPD drug claims for administered antibiotics for patients without a reported HAC provide some additional evidence that HACs related to infections are potentially unreported. Limiting the observation period for a hospital-acquired condition to just the hospitalization period may be too narrow, given the presence of these conditions in later inpatient claims and evidence of antibiotic treatment post-discharge.

Section 6. Summary and Conclusions

In this report, we have investigated the impact of three different HACs on the likelihood of readmission within 30 days and on the likelihood of discharge to a PAC setting. We used mixed effect logistic modeling to control for various other characteristics that may explain the likelihood of readmission and to account for the clustering of discharges within hospitals. The results suggest a very strong relationship between the presence of a HAC and the likelihood of both readmission and discharge to a PAC setting.

The relationship between the presence of a HAC and the likelihood of readmission within 30 days varied across the three HACs included in our analyses. For the falls and trauma HAC and the DVT/PE HAC, the presence of the HAC is associated with a 21 to 23% increase in the odds of being readmitted within 30 days. The presence of the vascular catheter-associated infection HAC has an even greater impact on the likelihood of readmission. It is associated with a 33% increase in the odds of being readmitted within 30 days.

The relationship between the presence of a HAC and the likelihood of discharge to a PAC setting also varied across the three HACs. The odds of being discharged to a PAC setting are 2.7 times greater for patients with the falls and trauma HAC, two times greater for patients with the catheter-associated infection HAC, and 40% greater for patients with the DVT/PE HAC compared to similar patients without the HACs. Discharge to a PAC setting does not appear to be mutually exclusive with a hospital readmission within 30 days. In fact, patients who were discharged to PAC settings were more likely to be readmitted within 30 days. This was true for patients with each of the HACs as well as for patients in our control groups.

And lastly, we examined the degree to which readmission estimation bias may be present in the Medicare claims data due to the presence of unreported HACs in the claims, using both physician claims linked to the hospital claim, and also 30 days of follow-up claims. We found that significant numbers of HAC-related conditions were reported on physician claims linked to hospital discharges where no HAC (or POA) was coded. These potentially unreported HACs could create bias in readmission estimations. There was fairly poor correspondence between HACs coded on the hospital claims and HAC-related conditions coded on the linked physician claims.

We examined physician claims linked to the hospital claims for the infection HACs and DVT/PE following certain orthopedic procedures, and found that, particularly for the SSIs, the time to clinical presentation of the infection can be more than a week, longer than the typical hospital stay for some of these surgical procedures. However, physician claims from infectious disease specialists identifying HAC-related conditions are common across many of the conditions studied during the hospitalization and could signal the presence of the infection where it is not otherwise identified on the hospital claim.

Significant numbers of HAC-related conditions are identified on inpatient claims within the 30 days following a hospitalization with the relevant HAC-related procedure or surgery. Outpatient claims data for administered antibiotics also points to potentially unreported HACs, or HAC-related conditions that manifest after the initial hospitalization.

References

Ashton, C.M., DelJunco, D.J., Souchek, J., et al.: The association between the quality of inpatient care and early readmission: a meta-analysis of the evidence. *Med. Care* 35(10):1044- 1059, October 1997.

Averill, R.F., McCullough, E.C., Hughes, J.S., et al.: Redesigning the Medicare Inpatient PPS to Reduce Payments to Hospitals with High Readmission Rates. *Health Care Financ. Rev.* 30(4):1-15, Summer 2009.

Baser, O., Supina, D., Sengupta, N., & Kwong, L. (2010). Impact of postoperative venous thromboembolism on Medicare recipients undergoing total hip replacement or total knee replacement surgery. *American Journal of Health-Systems Pharmacy,* 67, 1438-1445.

Beckman, M., Hooper, C., Critichley, S., & Ortel, T. (2010). Venous thromboembolism a public health concern. *American Journal of Preventive Medicine,* 38, S495-S501.

Carter, K., (2010). Identifying and managing deep vein thrombosis. *Primary Health Care,* 20, 30-39.

Encinosa, W.E., and Hellinger, F.J.: The impact of medical errors on ninety-day costs and outcomes: an examination of surgical patients. *HSR: Health Serv. Res.* 43(6):2067-2085, December 2008.

Friedman, B., and Basu, J.: The rate and cost of hospital readmissions for preventable conditions. *Med. Care Res. Rev.* 61(2):225-240, June 2004.

Friedman, B., Encinosa, W., Jiang, J.H., et al.: Do patient safety events increase readmissions? *Med. Care* 47(5):583-590, May 2009.

Fuji, T., Takahiro, O., Shigeo, N., et al. (2008). Prevention of postoperative venous thromboembolism in Japanese patients undergoing total hip or knee arthroplasty: two randomized, double-blind-placebo-controlled studies with three dosage regimens of enoxaparin. *Journal of Orthopaedic Science*, 13, 442-451.

Geerts, W., Bergqvist, D., Pineo, G. et al. (2008). Prevention of venous thromboembolism: American College of Chest Physicians evidence-based clinical practice guidelines (8th edition).*Chest*, 133 (6), (suppl): 381S-453S.

Goldfield, N.I., McCullough, E.C., Hughes, J.S., et al.: Identifying potentially preventable readmissions. *Health Care Financ. Rev.* 30(1):75-91, Fall 2008.

Haines, S. (2010). Improving the quality of care for patients at risk for venous thromboembolism. *American Journal of Health-System Pharmacy*, 67, S3-S8.

Herwaldt, L.A., Cullen, J.J., Scholz, D., et al.: A prospective study of outcomes, healthcare resource utilization, and costs associated with postoperative nosocomial infections. Infect. *Control Hosp. Epidemiol.* 27(12):1291-1298, December 2006.

Horwitz, L., Partovian, C., Lin, Z., et al.: *Hospital-Wide (All Condition) 30-Day Risk-Standardized Readmission Measure: Draft Measure Methodology Report.* Contract no. HHSM500-2008-0025I/HHSM-500-T0001, Modification No. 000005. New Haven, Conn.Yale New Haven Health Service Corporation/Center for Outcomes Research & Evaluation (YNHHSC/CORE), August 2011.

Huang S.S., Placzek H., Livingston J., et al. Use of Medicare claims to rank hospitals by surgical site infection risk following coronary artery bypass graft surgery. Infect. Control Hosp. Epidemiol. 2011 Aug;32(8):775-83.

Jencks, S.F., Williams, M.V., and Coleman, E.A.: Rehospitalizations among patients in the Medicare fee-for-service program. *N. Engl. J. Med.* 360(14):1418-1428, April 2009.

Kandilov, A., McCall, N., Dalton, K., and Miller, R.D. February 2012. *Readmissions Due to Hospital-Acquired Conditions (HACs).* Report prepared for Centers for Medicare and Medicaid Services Office of Research, Development, and Information under Contract no. HHSM-500-2005-000291. Research Triangle Park, NC: RTI International.

Kim, E., & Bartholomew, J. Venous Thromboembolism. Retrieved November 5, 2010 from http://www.clevelandclinicmeded.com/medicalpubs/disease management/cardiology/

Kohut, K. Guide for the Prevention of Mediastinitis Surgical Site Infections Following Cardiac Surgery. Association for Professionals in Infection Control and Epidemiology. 2008.

Lip, G., & Tse H. (2007). Management of atrial fibrillation. *Lancet*, 370, 604-618.

McNair, P. D., & Luft, H. S.: Enhancing Medicare's hospital-acquired conditions policy to encompass readmissions. *Medicare Care & Medicaid Res. Rev.* 2012; 2(2), E1-E15.

Morris, D.S., Rohrbach, J., Rogers, M., Sundaram, L.M.T., Sonnad, S., Pascual, J., Sarani, B., Reilly, P., and Sims, C.: The Surgical Revolving Door: Risk Factors for Hospital Readmission. *Journal of Surgical Research,* January 2011.

National Nosocomial Infections Surveillance (NNIS) System Report, data summary from January 1992 through June 2004, issued October 2004. *Am. J. Infect. Control* 2004; 32:470-85.

Rosenbaum, P.R., and Rubin, D.B.: The central role of the propensity score in observational studies for causal effects. *Biometrika* 70:41-55, 1983.

Peterson, E., Coombs, L., Ferguson, T., Shroyer, A., DeLong, E., Grover, F.,& Edwards, F., (2002). Hospital variability in length of stay after coronary artery bypass surgery: results from the Society of Thoracic Surgeons' National Cardiac Database. *Annals of Thoracic Surgery*, 74, 464-473.

Swenne, C.L., Linholm, C., Borowiec, J., Carlsson, M.: Surgical-site infections within 60 days of CABG, *J. Hosp. Infect.* (2004); 57(1):14-24 - Reported .5 - 5% within 60 days post discharge.

Wells, P., Borah, B., Sengupta, N., Supina, S., McDonald, H., & Kwong, L. (2010). Analysis of venous thromboprophylaxis duration and outcomes in orthopedic patients. *The American Journal of Managed Care*, 16, 857-866.

Zierler, B., Wittkowsky, A., Peterson, G., Lee, J., Jacobsen, C., Glenny, R., Wolf, F., Robins, L., Mitchell, P., Wolpin, S., Payne, T., Hendrie, P., Han, G., & Oh, H. (2008). Venous thromboembolism safety toolkit: a systems approach to patient safety. Retrieved June 26, 2012 from http://www.ahrq.gov/downloads/pub/advances2/vol3/Advances-Zierler 81.pdf.

End Notes

[1] See pages 29-30 of Horwitz et al. (2011) for a fuller description of the rationale for the creation of the comorbid risk variables.

[2] Interestingly, HAC rates fall for both falls and trauma and DVT/PE following certain orthopedic procedures between FY 2010 and FY 2011, despite the fact that more diagnosis codes are used in FY 2011. This could reflect a significant, system-wide reduction in these HACs that is larger than the effect of the increased number of diagnosis codes. It could also reflect that these HACs have a greater likelihood of facing a payment penalty, and thus

there is a greater incentive for under-reporting of these HACs. From Appendix 4, we see that more than one quarter of claims with a falls and trauma HAC face a payment penalty, and more than 40% of DVT/PE HAC claims face a payment penalty.

[3] 126 physician-identified mediastinitis cases + 69 mediastinitis HACs = 195 cases of mediastinitis. 126 physician-identified mediastinitis cases ÷ 195 mediastinitis cases = .646.

Index

M

N

O

P

Q

R

S

T

U

V

W

Y